Teaching for SUCCESSFUL INTELLIGENCE

*We dedicate this book to the many wonderful
teachers who have helped us develop the
material herein and deliver it to so many children.*

ROBERT J.
STERNBERG ELENA L.
GRIGORENKO

Teaching for
SUCCESSFUL
INTELLIGENCE

To Increase Student Learning
and Achievement

Skyhorse Publishing

Visit our website at www.skyhorsepublishing.com.

10 9 8 7 6 5 4 3 2 1

Library of Congress Cataloging-in-Publication Data is available on file.

Cover design by Monique Hahn and Michael Dubowe

Print ISBN: 978-1-63450-373-0
Ebook ISBN: 978-1-5107-0128-1

Printed in the United States of America

Contents

Introduction

WHY TEACH FOR SUCCESSFUL INTELLIGENCE?

People need all their skills to be operating in very good order to be successful in life. Yet many educational programs seem to develop people's intelligence in only one area—analytical intelligence—giving minimal or even no attention to two other areas of intelligence—creative and practical intelligence—that are just as vital to living successfully. Sternberg (1997, 1999) has identified analytical, creative, and practical thinking abilities as composing successful intelligence and has noted that successful people use all three abilities to achieve success. Being exceptional in one thinking skill may not be enough to be successful in life.

This book provides teachers with a series of lessons, based on a research-based theory, that use a number of proven techniques to promote development of all three abilities (Sternberg, Torff, & Grigorenko, 1998a, 1998b). This book is unusual in two ways. First, it is based quite closely on a particular theory of human intelligence—the theory of successful intelligence. Second, it is unusual because in hard empirical studies this theory has been shown to provide teaching and assessment techniques that work and that are superior to some of the major alternatives (Sternberg, Grigorenko, Ferrari, & Clinkenbeard, 1999; Sternberg, Grigorenko, & Jarvin, 2001). One such alternative is conventional teaching that emphasizes memory and critical thinking. Research shows that even if a teacher's only goal were to improve recall of factual knowledge, he or she would obtain better results by using the techniques in this book than by teaching for straight recall (Grigorenko, Jarvin, & Sternberg, 2002; Sternberg, 2002). If a teacher's goal is to improve analytical, creative, and practical thinking as related to the knowledge students acquire, this is the book to accomplish that goal. These techniques enable students to learn in ways that best suit them and thus cause them to be more motivated to learn.

WHO IS THIS BOOK FOR?

This book is written for teachers of kindergarten to twelfth grade, and even those at the college level, who want to improve their skills in teaching and assessment. It is written to give teachers both the basic theory they need to understand how to bring about this improvement and the specific detailed teaching and assessment techniques they need to apply the theory in their classrooms. This book includes numerous classroom examples of all techniques described.

This book was designed to be used. It is not only a reference, but also a primer in how to apply specific techniques in the classroom. For this reason, it encourages both passive and active learning. Teachers will gain full benefit from it only if they initiate active use of the materials.

HOW IS THIS BOOK ARRANGED?

Teaching for Successful Intelligence has three parts. Part I introduces the theory of successful intelligence and gives its underlying research support. After successful intelligence is defined in Chapter 1, empirical support for the theory is presented in Chapter 2. Chapter 3 provides the background on why teaching successful intelligence is so important and so difficult in the educational system in the United States today.

Part II concentrates on the three successful intelligence abilities—analytical, creative, and practical—and how teachers can foster these skills through classroom teaching. Lessons that aid in teaching each skill are presented in three chapters. Analytical thinking ability, which centers around the skills of problem solving and decision making, is presented in Chapter 4. This chapter comprises seven lessons that help students develop skills in individual problem-solving steps. In Chapter 5, creative thinking is presented from the viewpoint of making an investment, and thirteen lessons are provided to help teachers move their students from solving problems to creating ideas. Much of practical thinking ability, discussed in Chapter 6, is related to using common sense. Surprisingly, many people lack the ability to use common sense, so it is beneficial to study it in this context. Each lesson in Chapter 6 begins by presenting a challenge teachers may encounter, and, after discussion, provides techniques they can use to help students conquer this challenge. Each lesson in these three chapters includes suggestions for applying the lesson's concept to specific subject areas and identifies grade levels for the suggested activities. Each concludes with a short activity that provides readers with the opportunity to come up with examples of how they can use the techniques in the chapter to enhance their classroom practices.

Part III focuses on how teachers design and use instructional units that facilitate students' learning using the three thinking skills in the classroom. Chapter 7 concentrates on how teachers can develop triarchic instruction and assessment—successful intelligence—units. A step-by-step procedure is outlined and illustrated with numerous examples. Chapter 8, an extended illustration of a successful intelligence unit that has been used in a real classroom, gives readers the opportunity to see the whole that comes from the parts by providing examples of effectively taught lessons for successful intelligence.

About the Authors

 **Robert J. Sternberg** is currently Dean of the School of Arts and Sciences at Tufts University, where he is also Professor of Psychology. He was previously IBM Professor of Psychology and Education. Dr. Sternberg received his PhD from Stanford and is the recipient of eight honorary doctorates. In addition, he has won more than two dozen awards for his work. He is a former president of the American Psychological Association and the author of over 1,100 books, articles, and book chapters.

 **Elena L. Grigorenko** received her PhD in general psychology from Moscow State University and her PhD in developmental psychology and genetics from Yale University. She is currently Associate Professor of Child Studies and Psychology at Yale and Associate Professor of Psychology at Moscow State University. Dr. Grigorenko has published more than 200 peer-reviewed articles, book chapters, and books. She has received many professional awards, and her research has been funded by various federal and private organizations. Dr. Grigorenko has worked with children from around the world, including those living in Africa, Asia, Europe, and the Americas.

PART I

Understanding Successful Intelligence

In the opening chapters of the book, we present the reasoning and research that support the theory of successful intelligence and the success that students and teachers encounter when they develop skills in analytical, creative, and practical thinking. Since the educational systems in the United States don't often support successful intelligence abilities and assessment—analytical, creative, and practical—we hope these initial chapters provide a practical foundation that will lead to successful implementation in all levels of classrooms, from primary to college. Chapter 1 defines successful intelligence, while Chapter 2 provides support for the theory; Chapter 3 presents background information on the need to incorporate these skills into learning environments across grade levels.

What Is Successful Intelligence?

A GRIZZLY BEAR'S LUNCH

Two boys are walking in a forest. The two boys are quite different. The first boy's teachers think he is smart, his parents think he is smart, and, as a result, he thinks he is smart. He has excellent scores on both ability and achievement tests, excellent grades, and other notable paper credentials that should take him far in his scholastic life.

Few people consider the second boy smart. His test scores are nothing special, his grades are not so great, and his other credentials, though satisfactory, are not notable. At best, people would call him shrewd or street-smart.

As the two boys walk through the forest, they encounter a problem: A huge, ferocious, hungry-looking grizzly bear is charging straight at them. The first boy calculates that the grizzly bear will overtake them in 17.3 seconds. This is an impressive feat, given the strain they are under. Not only does this boy know the Distance = Rate × Time formula, but he is able to apply it under great duress. The second boy would never be able to calculate the number of seconds until impact, and would never try.

The first boy, panicking, looks over at the second boy, who is taking off his hiking boots and putting on jogging shoes. The first boy says to the second boy, "You must be crazy. There is no way we are going to outrun that grizzly bear!" The second boy replies, "That's true. But all I have to do is outrun you."

The outcome is that the first boy becomes the grizzly bear's lunch, and the second boy jogs off to safety. There is more to the story; you can find out what ultimately happens to the second boy at the end of this chapter.

DEFINING SUCCESSFUL INTELLIGENCE

This obviously fictitious vignette illustrates the concept of successful intelligence and how it differs from conventional intelligence.

Successful intelligence is the integrated set of abilities needed to attain success in life, however an individual defines it, within that individual's sociocultural context. People are successfully intelligent by recognizing their strengths and making the most of them at the same time that they recognize their weaknesses and find ways to correct or compensate for them. Successfully intelligent people adapt to, shape, and select environments by using a balance of analytical, creative, and practical abilities. The major elements of successful intelligence are described below.

Description of Successful Intelligence

1. The *set of abilities* a person needs to attain success in life, however the person defines it.

2. Success is defined only in terms of *sociocultural context*. It does not occur in the abstract, but rather with respect to standards or expectations held either personally or by others.

3. A person's ability to recognize and make the most of his or her *strengths*. Almost everyone is good at something.

4. A person's ability to recognize and compensate for or correct his or her *weaknesses*. No one is good at everything.

5. A person's ability to *adapt to, shape,* and *select environments* by adjusting thinking or behavior to fit better into the environment in which he or she is functioning or by choosing a new environment.

This lengthy description of successful intelligence can be further examined by referring back to the story of the two boys and the grizzly bear. The first boy, obviously, is conventionally intelligent; the second boy, successfully intelligent.

Set of Abilities

The set of abilities needed to attain success in an individual's life, however the individual defines success, is the first component of successful intelligence. Intelligence has traditionally been defined in terms of some kind of success. Historically, this success has been primarily scholastic. The grizzly bear vignette points out how it is possible to have the abilities needed to achieve success in school and yet be caught short when it comes to the abilities needed to attain success in life. Indeed, the first boy in the story literally dies. Thus, if a basic criterion of success is being able to stay alive, the first boy did not succeed; the second boy did.

However, note that there is no one definition of success. The first boy may have valued academic success highly, in which case he was successful during the course of his short life. If the second boy valued academic success, he was less successful, because he had not obtained any great achievement in school. But perhaps success in school never mattered much to him, as it does not matter much to many students. His street smarts may have carried him through the challenges in life that mattered most to him, just as street smarts help many people attain what they want in life.

The story of the grizzly bear is obviously apocryphal. But the difference between IQ-like abilities and practical abilities can be seen in countless real-world cases. This was epitomized in the words of a manager who once stated, "It is the fate of A students to be managed by B and C students." I was one of these C students and received a C when I took an introductory psychology course. Today, though, I have a successful career in a field in which I got a C in the introductory course.

Another example: Some years ago a department in a university acquired a new chairperson, about whom everyone was extremely excited. His career had been brilliant, and on top of that he was a world-renowned expert in management—exactly his mission for his new department. Unfortunately, he was a miserable manager. He was academically brilliant and a management expert, but he was not an expert manager. He could not practice his academic preaching. When he accepted a position elsewhere, his announcement was met with a universal sigh of relief and even rejoicing.

However, academic intelligence is not necessarily negatively correlated with success. A good example is Marilyn vos Savant, who is listed in the *Guinness Book of World Records* as having a record-breaking IQ, measured when she was a child. Over the past years, she has written a variety of books, which are perhaps distinguished for being so undistinguished. Neither they nor the columns she has written for a very popular magazine seem to demonstrate any great signs of the exceptionality some people might expect from her IQ. However, she has been extremely successful in marketing herself for her very high IQ. Thus, her success has been in turning her IQ itself to her advantage.

The Sociocultural Context

Success can be defined only in terms of a sociocultural milieu. It does not occur in the abstract; it occurs with respect to some set of standards or expectations, whether of oneself or of others.

The grizzly bear story is intended to illustrate that milieus that matter a great deal in a person's life may differ drastically from scholastic milieus. The first boy most likely would be more successful than the second in school, but he did not survive the real-world encounter with the grizzly bear.

The grizzly bear story also illustrates the extent to which successful intelligence always occurs within a range of contexts. Had the two boys not walked in a zone where there were grizzly bears, their life outcomes might have been completely different. In one environment, knowing when to run may be critical for survival, as many organisms—not just humans—have discovered through time. Some animals need to be able to run to escape predators, such as grizzly bears, or risk death. However, for animals in a mountainous region, successfully scaling mountain peaks and preventing oneself from falling might be more important skills for survival. In a war zone, knowing how to negotiate with enemy soldiers may mean the difference between life and death. Different skills matter in different environments.

The importance of sociocultural contexts shows up in teaching. As any experienced teacher knows, the strategies that work well in one context often do not work well in another. Even within a given country, widespread differences can exist. For example, the jokes that are thought to be funny in the East may not seem so funny in the Midwest, and vice versa.

Gaining behavioral compliance also may vary from one culture to another. Several years ago I was giving a lecture at the University of Puerto Rico and found myself confronting a serious classroom management problem: the professors of education in the audience just were not listening. For whatever reason, they had tuned me out and were walking around and out of the room, speaking among themselves, and generally being very inattentive.

I tried the standard, uncreative techniques everyone learns in the course of training to be a teacher, lowering my voice in the hope that these professors would then lower their voices so that they would be able to hear me. Of course, I was assuming that they wanted to hear, an assumption that proved to be false. Instead, they appeared to be grateful that I had lowered my voice so that they could hear themselves better. I then asked them to be quiet, but that did not work either. Finally, after I had given up, a woman in the audience stood up and said something in rapid-fire Spanish. After that, the room was completely silent, and the audience remained quiet and attentive for the rest of the session.

What did the woman say? She had capitalized on her understanding of the cultural context. Puerto Rico is primarily a shame culture, not a guilt culture. My attempts to make the audience feel guilty might have worked in the mainland United States, but they were ineffective in Puerto Rico. In contrast, the woman pointed out to the audience that if they continued to be noisy, I would leave with a poor impression of the University of Puerto Rico, which I then would report to others. She said that the audience had no right to convey a bad impression and thus cast shame on the university. This appeal achieved the behavioral change that I had sought unsuccessfully because I was unaware of the sociocultural context in which I was operating.

Building on Strengths

Another component of successful intelligence is the ability to recognize and make the most of strengths. Almost everyone is good at something, even while no one is good at everything. This is a key fact and is critical for an understanding of successful intelligence. Successfully intelligent people figure out what they do well and make the most of it. The street-smart boy shrewdly calculated not numbers but avenues of escape. It is quite possible that the first boy would have been able to use his academic skills to figure a way out of the situation, but he did not. Although he may have recognized his strength, he was not able to capitalize on it, and the result was that he was eaten.

In another kind of situation—for example, the classroom—the first boy might have capitalized on his strengths better than the second boy. Given that his grades were better, this conclusion seems likely. But the vignette also points out that different situations in life have different stakes, and the situations where a person's life is at stake are probably, more often than not, situations where practical skills play a larger role than do academic skills. At the same time, this may not always be true. If a person has to drive across a desert that has no fuel services, knowing how to calculate how far the car can go on a tank of gas could mean the difference between life and death.

This point has another important implication. Because no one is good at everything, there is no single road either to intelligence or to success. If a person thinks of a few top people in any field—say, the best teachers she has had—she inevitably finds that there is no pat formula for their success. If there were, many people would use it. A certain teacher may be particularly effective in lecturing, another in leading discussions, a third in guiding students in self-directed activities. They are all successful because they have found ways to capitalize on their strengths.

Once, while listening to a lecture by a well-known teacher in the field of teaching for thinking, I marveled at how well the teacher was able to establish rapport and communicate with the audience. I commented to the person sitting next to me that I wished I could deliver a lecture so effectively. She looked at me for a moment and then commented, "He does it his way; you do it your way." Her point was right on target. Each person has to find his or her own path. There is no one path that works for everyone.

Compensating for Weaknesses

Successful people also recognize and compensate for or correct weaknesses. No one is good at everything, and thus, everyone needs to learn how to cope with weaknesses.

Psychologists and educators can talk all they want about "general intelligence," but it is unlikely that they can find a person with no intellectual weaknesses, no matter the person's IQ. People succeed in life not because they are free of weaknesses, but because they know what their weaknesses are and how to correct or compensate for them. Those who do not recognize these weaknesses pay a heavy price, no matter how outstanding their strengths may be.

Adapting, Shaping, and Selecting Environments

Another important component of successful intelligence is the ability to adapt to, shape, and select environments. People adapt to environments when they modify their thinking or their behavior to fit better into their environments. For example, students need to adapt to school contexts even if they want to think or do things that do not conform to the demands of the school. Teachers tend to value students who adapt well because such students meet the teachers' expectations for classroom behavior. To meet a school's procedures and standards, teachers need to adapt to school environments. In a similar way, principals tend to value teachers who adapt to their expectations.

The traditional definition of intelligence emphasizes the importance of adaptation to the environment (e.g., Binet & Simon, 1916; Wechsler, 1939). However, when viewed in a broad sense, successful intelligence involves more than just adaptation. Sometimes an individual decides that the intelligent thing to do is not to adapt to the environment, but rather to attempt to shape it. For example, a teacher in a school environment that encourages rote memorization might decide that instruction exclusively emphasizing rote memorization is not in the best interests of his students. The teacher might attempt to shape the environment, changing it to suit his beliefs or values.

When a person attempts to shape the environment, he is risking disagreement with those in power more than when he adapts to the environment. A shaper's superior(s) may not look happily upon or accept his thinking or actions. A student attempting to shape the environment might lose the goodwill of his teacher, and a teacher attempting to shape the environment may lose the goodwill of his principal. In extreme cases, the teacher might lose his job. People attempting to shape their environment need to be aware of the price they may have to pay.

Successful intelligence involves a balance between adaptation and shaping. On the one hand, someone who always adapts and never attempts to shape seems to be extremely conforming and, in some cases, lacking in principles or at least in character and gumption. Someone who always shapes, however, is often quickly viewed as counterproductive, divisive, or even obstructionistic. Successfully intelligent people thus decide which battles are worth fighting, and fight them; otherwise, they adapt. By making informed choices, they signal their willingness to be both creative and adaptive in their environments.

There is more to successful intelligence than adapting and shaping, however. Sometimes the optimal option is to leave one environment and select another. A person may decide that a job, a relationship, a place to live, or anything else is no longer serving (or never really did serve) a viable purpose. Perhaps the organization for which a person works requires her to do things she considers unethical. Or perhaps the flame that once lit up a relationship is now merely a dying flicker. In some cases, a person may choose to move on. In other cases, someone else may decide for the person, as when a supervisor loses confidence that an employee is carrying out the supervisor's vision of what needs to be done in the workplace.

An example of environmental selection is depicted in the movie *The Dead Poets' Society*. Played by Robin Williams, John Keating, a teacher who tries to make the subject of English come alive for his students, is at odds with the stuffy norms of the school in which he teaches. It becomes clear that there is no room for a Keating-type teacher in that school, so the only question is whether such a teacher will resign or be pushed out.

Successful intelligence involves a balance among adaptation, shaping, and selection. In most cases, people first try to make an environment work for them by adapting or shaping. But if attempts fail, selecting a new environment may be the best option.

THE TRIARCHY OF THINKING ABILITIES

As mentioned, the three abilities that make up successful intelligence are analytical, creative, and practical. *Analytical ability* is used when a person analyzes, evaluates, compares, or contrasts. *Creative ability* is used when a person creates, invents, or discovers. *Practical ability* is used when a person puts into practice, applies, or uses what he or she has learned. These three abilities are discussed in further detail in Chapters 4, 5, and 6. Successfully intelligent people show a balance of these three kinds of thinking. In schools, much of the thinking expected of students is of the analytical kind. But out of school and in the real world, creative and especially practical abilities may become much more important.

Consider the components of successful intelligence in an example from the life of a teacher. Such examples are common and occur on a daily basis.

Mrs. Quinn is a first-grade teacher who takes her responsibility to teach her students reading seriously (see Sternberg & Spear-Swerling, 1996). She wants and expects all students to learn to read. She believes that her task is made more difficult by the basal reading program her school has adopted and that all teachers at all grade levels are expected to use. This basal program—a program consistent with the district philosophy—is based exclusively on a whole-language approach to teaching reading. This approach emphasizes teaching whole words rather than phonics and teaching these words in naturalistic contexts.

Mrs. Quinn herself advocates this approach, but not exclusively. She finds it ironic that twenty-five years ago, in the same district and in the same school, she was forced to use a basal series that placed essentially exclusive emphasis on phonics, an emphasis she did not like either. Many reading specialists, such as Mrs. Quinn, advocate a more balanced approach (e.g., Adams, 1990; Stanovich, 1999; Sternberg & Grigorenko, 1999). Meanwhile, Mrs. Quinn is finding that although the basal program works well for some students, it does not work well for others. What should she do?

In attempting to solve this problem, Mrs. Quinn engages the same elements of successful intelligence that all people use in much of their everyday problem solving. For her, success means, in part, teaching students to read well. Her definition of success makes sense in the socio-cultural context in which she works. She is, after all, a first-grade teacher.

Mrs. Quinn knows that she has the ability to teach the students, but she also knows that she cannot do it alone. Her strength is in motivating students and in helping them become excited about reading. Mrs. Quinn knows how to make the most of her strength. She reads to the students orally, and her active, lively inflection combined with her ability to make students feel as if they are part of the action excites students about reading. However, Mrs. Quinn also knows that she is not as strong on the technical side and that she, like most teachers, needs a lot of support from a strong reading program of some kind. Thus, Mrs. Quinn uses the teaching manual of the basal to compensate for what she perceives to be her weakness in the technical arena. But Mrs. Quinn is not convinced that the reading program, even with the teaching manual adopted by the school district, is a particularly strong one—at least not for many of the students whom she teaches.

Mrs. Quinn has decided to modify the program by using some of the phonics techniques she learned when she used a primarily phonics-based approach in her teaching. Thus, she balances adapting to and shaping of the environment. She uses the basal reading program the district requires (adapting), but supplements the lessons extensively with additional techniques (shaping). However, she goes beyond just using the techniques she has learned in the past. Because she has found that many students get bored with pure phonics, she uses another personal skill and sets the phonics lessons to music. She sings and has the students sing along with her. The melodies help the students remember what they have learned. Mrs. Quinn's creative approach helps her in achieving a very practical goal—helping students learn to read.

CONCLUSION

Successful intelligence is the integrated set of abilities needed to attain success in life, however a person defines it, within his or her sociocultural context. People are successfully intelligent by recognizing their strengths and making the most of them while at the same time recognizing their weaknesses and finding ways to correct or compensate for them. Successfully intelligent people manifest their skills by adapting to, shaping, and selecting environments through a balance in their use of analytical, creative, and practical abilities. Teachers and students alike employ successful intelligence every day—inside and outside the classroom. In doing so, they go well beyond the conventional definition of intelligence.

Returning to the story of the two boys and the grizzly bear in the forest, what happened to the second boy? The second boy, after experiencing the death of his friend, acquired a phobia of forests. However, because he was practically intelligent, he realized he could not spend the rest of his life that way. So he learned modern techniques for fighting phobias, such as deep relaxation and self-hypnosis. Then, he returned to the forest.

He discovered, to his delight, that his phobia was conquered. He felt relaxed and at peace with nature. At this point, he learned a cruel lesson. Whereas lightning never strikes twice in the same place, grizzly bears do. As the second boy was relaxing, the same grizzly bear returned and charged after him. It was starved, not having eaten a decent meal since it ate the first boy.

The second boy was frightened, realizing that he no longer had the option of outrunning another boy. Not being able to think of any other alternative, he got down on his knees and started to pray. He prayed that the grizzly bear would become a good, religious being like himself. It may sound farfetched, but just as the grizzly bear was about to attack the second boy and eat him alive, it got down on its haunches and started to pray too.

The point of this chapter has been that creative and practical intelligence tend to be undervalued in schools. But that it is not to say that traditional, academic, analytical abilities are unimportant. Of course, they are important too. And unfortunately, the second boy did not quite analyze the problem correctly. He did not think to specify the religion.

The grizzly bear, who had adopted a pagan religion, prayed, "I thank thee, oh gods, for the offering I am about to receive," and ate the second boy.

The point, of course, is that in life, a person needs a balance of all three types of abilities: analytical, creative, and practical.

The next chapter addresses whether the theory of successful intelligence works in the classroom and discusses why conventional notions of intelligence seem to be prevalent even when they are not very useful.

Examining the Theory of Successful Intelligence

DOES SUCCESSFUL INTELLIGENCE WORK IN THE CLASSROOM?

There are an awful lot of theories around. Some of them have been applied in a number of classrooms. Almost none of them have hard data showing their efficacy. But the theory of successful intelligence, in contrast to most theories applied in classrooms, is backed by hard data. Thus, the techniques presented in this book have been shown to work. Consider some of the studies that demonstrate the effectiveness of these techniques.

In one set of studies (Sternberg, Ferrari, Clinkenbeard, & Grigorenko, 1996; Sternberg, Grigorenko, Ferrari, & Clinkenbeard, 1999), researchers studied the question of whether conventional education in schools systematically discriminates against students with creative and practical strengths. Motivating this work was the belief that the systems in schools tend to strongly favor students with strengths in memory and analytical abilities.

A test for analytical, creative, and practical abilities, including both multiple-choice and essay items, was devised for high school students. The multiple-choice items required three kinds of thinking in three content domains: verbal, quantitative, and figural. Thus, there were nine multiple-choice and three essay subtests. The test was administered in the United States and in other countries to 326 students identified by their schools as gifted according to any standards the schools chose.

Students were selected for a summer program in college-level psychology if they fell into one of five ability groupings: high analytical, high creative, high practical, high balanced (high in all three abilities), or low balanced (low in all three abilities). These 199 selected students used the same introductory psychology textbook, a preliminary version of *In Search of the Human Mind* (Sternberg, 1995), and attended the same psychology lectures but were assigned to four different discussion sections reflecting different instructional conditions. These four instructional conditions were memory, analytical, creative, and practical. For example, in the memory instructional condition, students might be asked to describe the main tenets of a major theory of depression. In the analytical condition, they might be asked to compare and contrast two theories of depression. In the creative condition, they might be asked to formulate their own theory of depression. In the practical condition, they might be asked how they could use what they learned about depression to help a friend who was depressed.

All students were evaluated in terms of their performance on homework, a midterm exam, a final exam, and an independent project. Each type of work was evaluated for memory, analytical, creative, and practical quality. Thus, all students were evaluated in exactly the same way.

The results suggest the utility of the theory of successful intelligence. First, it was noted that students in the high creative and high practical groups were much more diverse in terms of racial, ethnic, socioeconomic, and educational backgrounds than were students in the high analytical group. In other words, just by expanding the range of abilities measured, more intellectual strengths than would have been apparent through a conventional test were discovered. Moreover, the students identified as strong differed in terms of the population from which they were drawn in comparison with students identified as strong solely in analytical measures.

The so-called general factor of intelligence was found to be very weak, suggesting that the general factor is probably relevant only when measuring a fairly narrow range of abilities, as is typically the case with conventional tests. It was found that the testing format had a large effect on results. Multiple-choice tests tended to correlate with other multiple-choice tests, almost without regard to what they measured. However, essay tests showed only weak correlations with multiple-choice tests. Furthermore, after controlling for modality of testing (multiple-choice versus essay), correlations among analytical, creative, and practical sections were found to be very weak and generally not statistically significant, thus supporting the relative independence of the various abilities. It was found that all three ability tests—analytical, creative, and practical— significantly predicted course performance. In all analyses, at least two of these ability measures contributed significantly to the prediction of each of the measures of achievement. One of the significant predictors of course performance was always the analytical score; perhaps this reflects the difficulty of de-emphasizing the analytical way of teaching. However, in a replication of the study with low-income African American students from New York, Deborah Coates (personal communication, 1998) found a different pattern of results. Her data indicated that the practical tests were better predictors of course performance than were the analytical measures, suggesting that the criterion each ability test predicts depends on population as well as mode of teaching.

Most important, an aptitude-treatment interaction was noted; students who were placed in instructional conditions that better matched their pattern of abilities outperformed students for whom instruction and abilities were mismatched. In other words, when students are taught in a way that fits how they think, they do better in school. Students with creative and practical abilities who are almost never taught or assessed in a way that matches their pattern of abilities may be at a disadvantage, course after course, year after year.

In a follow-up study, Sternberg, Torff, and Grigorenko (1998a, 1998b) looked at the learning of social studies and science by third-graders and eighth-graders. The third-graders were students in a very low income neighborhood in Raleigh, North Carolina. The eighth-graders were students from largely middle- to upper-middle classes studying in Baltimore, Maryland, and Fresno, California. In this study, students were assigned to one of three instructional conditions. In the first condition, students were taught the course as it would have been taught had the study not intervened. The emphasis was on memory. In a second condition, they were taught in a way that emphasized critical (analytical) thinking. In the third condition, they were taught in a way that emphasized analytical, creative, and practical thinking. Performances of all students were assessed for memory learning (through multiple-choice assessments) as well as for analytical, creative, and practical learning (through performance assessments). The amount of teaching time was the same across conditions.

As expected, it was found that students in the successful intelligence (analytical, creative, and practical) condition outperformed the other students in terms of the performance assessments. A person could argue that this result merely reflected the way these students were taught. Nevertheless, this result suggested that teaching for these kinds of thinking succeeded. More important, however, students in the successful intelligence condition outperformed the other students, even on the multiple-choice memory tests. In other words, to the extent that a teacher's goal is just to maximize students' memory for information, teaching for successful intelligence is still the superior practice. It enables students to capitalize on their strengths, to correct or to compensate for their weaknesses, and to encode material in a variety of interesting ways.

Thus, results from two sets of studies suggest that the theory of successful intelligence is valid not only in its parts, but also as a whole. Moreover, the results suggest that the theory can make a difference in laboratory tests as well as in school classrooms.

WHY ARE CONVENTIONAL NOTIONS OF INTELLIGENCE STILL PREVALENT?

Despite studies showing that a blend of analytical, creative, and practical abilities is what comprises successful intelligence, many schools still embrace outdated traditional notions of intelligence. Several reasons underlie the continuation of such notions of intelligence.

The Vicious Effects of Closed Systems

A narrow conception of intelligence seems to be prevalent in today's society because of what is referred to as a closed system. A *closed system* is self-contained, internally consistent, and difficult to escape. A closed system, once it is in place, becomes self-perpetuating and difficult to change.

The World According to Herrnstein and Murray

The vicious circle perpetuated by such a system gave rise to *The Bell Curve* (Herrnstein & Murray, 1994), a book that looks at the history of intelligence and class structure in the United States.

According to Herrnstein and Murray (1994), conventional tests of intelligence, on average, account for about 10 percent of the variation in various kinds of real-world outcomes. Although this percentage is not trivial, it is not particularly large either, and one might wonder what all the fuss is about in the use of the tests. Of course, one might argue that Herrnstein and Murray have underestimated the percentage, but given their enthusiastic support for conventional tests, it seems unlikely they would underestimate the value of the tests.

In fact, they may overestimate the value of the tests for predictive purposes. Clearly the tests have some value. But how much? In their book, Herrnstein and Murray (1994) refer to an "invisible hand of nature" that guides events so that people with high IQs tend to rise toward the top socioeconomic stratum of a society and people with low IQs tend to fall toward the bottom stratum. They present data to support their argument, and indeed it seems likely that, although many aspects of their data may be arguable (Fraser, 1995; Jacoby & Glauberman, 1995), in U.S. society their argument holds true. For example, on average, lawyers and doctors probably have higher IQs than do street cleaners.

The problem is that although the data are probably correct, the theory behind the data is probably not. U.S. society is not as it is because of an invisible hand of nature, but rather because a closed system has been created. The United States and some other societies have created cultures in which test scores matter profoundly. High test scores are needed for placement in higher tracks in elementary and secondary schools. They are needed for admission to selective undergraduate programs. They are needed again for admission to selective graduate and professional programs. It is really quite difficult to imagine how a person could gain access to many of the highest-paying and most prestigious jobs if he or she did not test well. Low scores exclude students from many selective colleges. Low Graduate Record Examination (GRE) scores tend to exclude students not only from one selective graduate school, but also from many others as well. Of course, test scores are not the only criterion used for admission to graduate and professional schools. But they count enough that if a person bombs one of the admissions tests, he or she can say good-bye to admission to many selective schools.

The 10 percent figure of Herrnstein and Murray (1994) implies that IQ-like abilities matter some, but not much, for life success. Other abilities may be more important. Many able people are disenfranchised because, although their abilities might be important for job performance, they are not important for test performance. For example, the creative and practical skills that matter to success on the job typically are not measured on tests used to get into school. Society may be overvaluing a fairly narrow range of skills, even if that range of skills may not serve individuals particularly well on the job.

The Role of Selection

It is scarcely surprising that ability tests predict school grades, because the tests were originally designed explicitly for this purpose (Binet & Simon, 1916). This makes how the United States and some other societies have created closed systems more obvious. Certain abilities are valued in instruction, such as memory and analytical abilities. Ability tests are then created that measure these abilities and predict school performance. Then, assessments of achievement are designed that also assess these abilities. Thus, it's little wonder that ability tests are more predictive in school than in the workplace. Within the closed system of the school, a narrow range of abilities leads to success on ability tests, in instruction, and on achievement tests. But these same abilities are less important later in life in the workplace.

Closed systems can be and have been constructed to value almost any set of attributes. In some societies, caste is the valued attribute. Members of certain castes are allowed to rise to the top; members of other castes have little or no chance. Of course, the members of the successful castes believe they are getting their due, much as the nobility in the Middle Ages did when they rose to the top and subjugated their serfs. Even in the United States, the IQ of a person born a slave in the early 1800s would make little difference—he or she would die a slave. Slave owners and others rationalized the system, as social Darwinists always have, by believing that the fittest were in the roles they rightfully deserved.

The mechanism of a closed system can be illustrated by the fact that any attribute at all can be selected. Suppose a society wished to select for height. Only those with the greatest height would be admitted to the highest tracks in schools, the most selective programs, and the most prestigious undergraduate programs. Shorter people would have to enroll in less prestigious programs and places. Elevator shoes, of course, would be forbidden in testing for height, in much the same way that cheating on tests is currently forbidden. Height standards for graduate admissions would be the most rigorous of all. Eventually the society would find that people in the top socioeconomic stratum tended to be very tall. People in the bottom stratum would tend to be very short.

Lest this all sound hypothetical, it is important to realize that society does select for height. Chief executive officers, army generals, and others in positions of power tend to be taller than the people they supervise. The example of height points out that, regardless of the society, attributes other than intelligence are going to matter for success. These attributes may include height, ethnic group, and interpersonal attractiveness, as well as personal attributes including diverse aspects of personality, motivation, emotion, and so forth.

In general, closed systems seal off individual options and distort society, depriving many individuals of opportunities they should have. Society is also deprived of their talents. Using conventional intelligence-based measures is probably better than using height or many other such measures, but society can likely do better by expanding the abilities for which it tests.

Attributes that have nothing to do with intelligence (at least, according to the present and most other definitions) can end up becoming conflated with intelligence. For example, I attended classes in a number of one-room elementary schools in Jamaica. In a typical school, there was no barrier separating the many classes in the single room, so the noise level was constantly high. I found myself asking what Binet might have put on his intelligence test if he had formulated his tests for these schools. I concluded that Binet might have decided to include in his test a battery of tests on hearing. This skill seemed most important for hearing the instruction and the test items, both of which typically were delivered verbally. In this situation, the students who heard better fared better, and those who did not hear well fared worse, especially if they had the bad fortune not to be sitting in the front center of the classroom.

The importance of hearing as related to intelligence is not just hypothetical. When I mentioned my observation in a colloquium, an individual from Guyana commented that she had grown up in similar schools and had always wondered why the smartest students sat in the front of the class. In this case, sitting in the front of the class may well have made students appear smart. The teacher probably did not think that good auditory (sensory hearing) abilities were a component of intelligence, but he or she might have easily conflated the effects of such abilities with intelligence. Similarly, students with poor vision who do not have the benefit of corrective lenses may also appear not to be very bright.

The experience in Jamaica also points out one other important fact, namely, that the (false) assumption in much research on intelligence is that all students have an equal chance to succeed on ability tests and in school. In fact, they do not. For example, in a study done in Jamaica, Sternberg, Powell, McGrane, and Grantham-McGregor (1997) studied the effects of intestinal parasitic infections (most often, whipworm) on students' cognitive functioning. Students with moderate to high levels of intestinal parasites tended to perform more poorly in school, and the researchers were interested in why this was the case. The study revealed that infected students tended to do more poorly on tests of higher-order cognitive abilities, even after controlling for possible confounding variables such as socioeconomic class. The data also revealed that, although antiparasitic medication improved physical health, it had no effect on cognitive ability test scores. Presumably, the deficits that were occurring had built up over many years and were not alleviated by a quick-fix pill. Students who are parasitically infected find it hard to concentrate on their schoolwork because they do not feel well. The data showed that the cumulative effect of missing much of what happens in school probably cannot be reversed quickly. Students in all societies with problems of health, poor nutrition, or questionable safety do not have equal chances to succeed.

The general conclusion is that societies can and do choose a variety of criteria to sort people. Some societies use caste systems, whether explicit, as in India, or implicit, as in the United States. Others use or have used race, religion, or wealth of parents as a basis for sorting. Many societies combine criteria. After a system is in place, those who gain access to the power structure, whether via their passage through elite education or otherwise, are likely to look for others similar to themselves to place in positions of power. The reason, quite simply, is that there probably is no more powerful basis of interpersonal attraction than similarity (see Sternberg, 1998), so that people in a power structure look for others similar to themselves. The result is a potentially endlessly looping closed system.

Self-Fulfilling Prophecies

The worst effect of closed systems is that they create self-fulfilling prophecies.

As an elementary school student, I failed miserably on the IQ tests I had to take. I was incredibly test-anxious. Just the sight of the school psychologist coming into the classroom to give a group IQ test sent me into a wild panic attack. And by the time the psychologist said "Go!" to get the class started, I was in such a funk that I could hardly answer any of the test items. I still remember being on the first couple of problems when the other students were already turning the page as they sailed through the test. For me, the game of taking the test was all but over before it even started. And the outcome was always the same: I lost.

Of course, countless test publishers, teachers, administrators, and school psychologists will swear that there is no such thing as "failing" an IQ test, that no one can "win" or "lose" on an IQ test. Maybe not, but for all practical purposes, if a person does not do well on the test, he or she loses the game, because failing results in that person's being labeled dumb.

It does not take a genius to figure out what happens next to students who do not do well on IQ tests. No one expects much from them. My early-elementary teachers certainly did not expect much from me. So I gave them what they expected. I was not a very good student in my first three years of elementary school. Were my teachers disappointed? Not on your life. They were happy that I was giving them what they expected, and I was just as happy that they were happy. So everyone was happy, and I was just one more loser in the game of life.

Was my low achievement because I just did not have the gray matter to be a high achiever, or was it in fact a self-fulfilling prophecy resulting from the teachers' knowledge of my IQ score? Most of the time, people never really find out, because students who start down the road to low achievement quickly discover that it is a one-way street to the academic twilight zone. And, as in the television show by that name, few people who enter the twilight zone ever leave it.

I was lucky in a way few students are. In fourth grade, at nine years of age, I ended up in Mrs. Alexa's class. Whereas my teachers in the early primary grades had all been deeply dug into the trenches of the testing field, Mrs. Alexa did not know or did not care much about IQ test scores. She believed I could do much better than I was doing, and she expected more. In fact, she demanded more of me. And she got it. Why? Because I wanted to please her, even more than I had wanted to please my teachers in the first three grades.

Mrs. Alexa did not seem particularly surprised, but I was astonished when I actually exceeded her expectations. I became a straight-A student very quickly. For the first time, I saw myself as someone who could be an A student, and thereafter, I was one. At the time, it never occurred to me that I had become an A student *because* I was smart; on the contrary, I felt certain that I had become an A student *in spite of* my low intelligence, as witnessed by my low test scores.

This kind of experience is not limited to the 1950s. For example, in the 1980s, thirty years after my own soporific adventures with Dick, Jane, and Sally, my son, Seth, was an elementary school student. Seth was in a good school, but, because of a move, transferred to another good school. The schools were very similar in every respect, right down to their physical appearances. For Seth, however, there was one stunning difference. In the first school he had been in the top reading group, whereas in the second school he was in the bottom reading group. It was hard for me to believe that a child could have lost so much intelligence just by moving during the summer.

What happened was that when Seth arrived at his new school, the school needed to place him in a reading group. The new school was not going to just take the word of the first school that Seth was in the top reading group. Instead, the school took what it viewed to be a more scientific approach. The first day of school, they gave Seth a test of reading ability. (Reading tests correlate pretty highly with tests of intellectual ability.) Seth bombed the test. Of course, it was Seth's first day in a new school, in a new building, with a new teacher and new students, not to mention the other adjustments that go with moving to and living in a new house. Seth was scarcely in a position to concentrate seriously on any kind of test at all. So it really was no surprise that he did not do well.

The effect of the low score was immediate and profound. Seth was placed in the lowest reading group. But after a while, Seth's teacher noticed that he was reading better than other students in the group, an observation that was scarcely surprising given that Seth had learned the skills being taught this group at his previous school. A person might think that because of this, the school would bump him up to the middle reading group. Instead, Seth was given the reading test again.

This time, his performance was better. He scored at a higher level on the reading test, so he was placed in the middle reading group. Soon, Seth's teacher noticed that he was reading better than the students in the middle reading group, and so, by the same logic, he was given the reading test again. And this time, he scored at the level of the students in the high reading group. Although my wife at the time and I, as Seth's parents, thought we could guess what the school would do next, we guessed wrong.

Seth was left in the middle reading group. We could not understand why his teachers took the scores on the reading test to be divine revelations the first two times but the third time crassly ignored the score. At a parent-teacher conference, the principal, the school psychologist, and the reading teacher all explained their actions. Although Seth indeed had done well on the reading test, he was now a full book behind the students in the top group. If he were advanced to the top group, he would miss all the skills in that book.

Talk about self-fulfilling prophecies! Because Seth had been distracted on his first day in his new school, he had been placed in a low-level reading group with low-level expectations, and as far as the school was concerned, he was now stuck. Multiply what happened to Seth by a few hundred million or so. That is a good picture of what is happening to students in schools all over the United States in a given year. Some schools start with low expectations, act in a way to generate those expectations, get what is expected, and "confirm" what was believed in the first place.

The underlying message in Seth's predicament was that the test—the predictor of reading performance—was more important than the performance it was supposed to predict, which was reading. It would be rather like saying that a forecast tells us more about the weather than does the weather itself. If the weather forecaster says it is going to rain, then that is what matters, not whether it actually rains.

This kind of backward logic is not limited to underachievement. Society sometimes refers to people whose achievement is higher than is expected from their IQ as overachievers. Again, the predictor becomes more important than the achievement itself, and instead of acknowledging that there is something wrong with the test, society concludes that there must be something wrong with the person.

The Role of Environment

In predicting failure, people sometimes grossly underestimate the difficulties faced by students, especially if they come from a lower socioeconomic class rather than a middle class such as Seth's environment. Many teachers, having grown up in the middle class, cannot imagine the duress under which many students live.

In some places, students' first preoccupation has to be their safety. They feel constantly threatened, and often justifiably so. In other cases, they are hungry or ill, as mentioned earlier. People must ask themselves how well they would be able to function under the conditions in which some students must function. While visiting Lucknow, India, the authors found an example of what conditions can do to students.

It was 113 degrees in the shade, but the students were sitting in the midday sun. The dozen or so students in the daycare in Lucknow, India, had been there all morning. As visitors, the authors had been there perhaps thirty minutes, but already were exhausted.

The setting was appalling. The movement of the students in the outdoor center was highly confined because their quarters were so cramped. Sitting on thin rugs, they were jammed into a small open space, perhaps the size of a typical bathroom in a middle-class home in the United States. Unfortunately, the analogy is apropos in more ways than one. The smell of excrement—human and animal—was everywhere. The sewer system was open; sewage was on the dirt streets, on the walkways, in the buildings. Human noses are supposed to stop noticing the smell after a time, but the stench never seemed to go away.

A number of similar settings can be found in Venezuela, Jamaica, Tanzania, Kenya, and elsewhere, so this setting is not unusual. It is better than some places, and worse than others. Similar environments can be found even in the United States.

Indirectly, the sewage was the reason for the visit. At a given time, roughly 40 percent of the students were infected with intestinal parasites, which are usually passed on through fecal contamination of food and drinking water or through the eating of dirt. The authors were in Lucknow to pilot test items that were to be used to assess the effects of medical deworming on cognitive functioning. The site of the study was one of more than 250 such sites in Lucknow.

In previous research, it had been found that intestinal worm infections are associated with reduced performance on complex cognitive tasks. Lest the problem sound arcane, according to the World Health Organization more than one billion children around the world are estimated to be infected with intestinal parasites (Stephenson, 2001). These infections can cost children an estimated 20 percent of what would have been their life span had they not been infected.

The combined effects of these infections and malnutrition are immediately noticeable. Sixty percent of all students in Lucknow are underweight, but in the slums of the study site, almost all the students were emaciated. Many had skin infections. One student was sweating profusely, all of the students were listless, and several of them looked ill. By age five, 3 percent of the slum students will have died (Stephenson, 2001). Many others will be severely compromised with respect to both health and nutrition. In the afternoon they will return to their homes, where usually there are no radios, no televisions, no toys, no books. The daycare center also lacks these items, as well as desks, chairs, tables, running water, and even a roof.

Grigorenko selected some of the older students. She asked them cognitive test questions. I, meanwhile, observed their performance, all of which was being translated from Hindi to English. After a time, Grigorenko posed a three-term series problem about the respective heights of three students: David is taller than Mary; Mary is taller than William; who is tallest? I whispered to her, "Isn't that problem unsolvable?" The student answered and the translator nodded that she got it right. Minus one for me. I could no longer think straight in the intensity of the 113-degree, humid, smelly heat. Could most people?

In judging students, teachers need to constantly think of how things look from the students' point of view. Too often, society has not done so, instead looking at things from the perspective of the school or the employer.

Successful Intelligence in Life and in School

SUCCESSFUL INTELLIGENCE IN LIFE: THE CHANGING DEMANDS OF THE LARGER WORLD

People today are living in an increasingly dynamic world—a world of changing technologies, changing economies, and changing job demands. The dominant slogan of the current employment policy seems to be "No long term." The traditional career path, in which an individual progresses step by step up the ladder of one or two jobs, has been increasingly deserted. The traditional deployment of a single set of skills through the course of a working life is withering.

Sociological research shows that as of the late 1990s a young U.S. resident with at least two years of college could expect to change jobs at least eleven times in the course of working and to change his or her skill base at least three times during those forty years of labor (Sennett, 1998). Permanent positions are being replaced by short-term contracts. Ongoing, full-time jobs are being replaced by projects and fields of work. In real life, the "no long term" mentality means that individuals must constantly look for jobs, keep moving, and be flexible, innovative, and resourceful. In the domain of abilities, the "no long term" mentality means that individuals must be analytical, creative, and practical; individuals must constantly analyze situations, use inner resources in an innovative way, and adapt to new workplaces.

If individuals accept that the modern labor world makes analytical, creative, and practical abilities not only a matter of preference but also a matter of necessity, then it is only logical to conclude that the mastery of

25

analytical, creative, and practical skills must be an important outcome of education.

SUCCESSFUL INTELLIGENCE IN SCHOOL: GIVING EVERYBODY A FAIR CHANCE

Years spent in school constitute a major portion of life and forever shape an individual. Most people remember many school successes and failures for the rest of their lives. Therefore, as educators, teachers want to maximize the probability of each student's success in school. The best way for them to achieve this outcome is to structure a wide range of activities so that students have a chance to try different patterns of abilities, discover their strongest abilities, and master, as much as they can, all of them. The hard question is how to do this for students with different combinations of skills. In the following scenarios, Alice, Barbara, and Celia represent students who each have a unique pattern of abilities. (All of these scenarios represent real situations, but the names are changed.)

Alice, the Analytical Thinker

Alice was the teacher's dream. She scored high on tests, performed well in class, and in general did everything a teacher would expect a bright student to do. The result was that Alice was always considered to be at or near the top of her class. Her high test scores were accepted as a valid indication of her ability to do outstanding work throughout her academic career. Yet by the time Alice was finished with graduate school in psychology, she was performing at a very modest level. About 70 to 80 percent of her classmates were doing better than she was.

Alice types occur at all levels of schooling. They are characterized by (a) high grades, (b) high test scores, (c) a general liking for school, (d) being liked by teachers, (e) fitting well into the school setting, (f) following directions, (g) seeing flaws in ideas, particularly those of others, (h) being natural "critics," and (i) preferring to be directed rather than structure their own learning.

The question that naturally arises is what went wrong with Alice, and what might go wrong with someone like her. The answer, quite simply, is that although Alice was excellent at remembering and analyzing other people's ideas, she was not very good at coming up with ideas of her own. Consequently, she faltered in advanced schooling, where (as in life) it is necessary for individuals to come up with ideas of their own. Similarly, although any highly analytical student is likely to have impressive academic skills, students need more than just a high level of academic achievement to do well in advanced schooling and in life.

Thomas is a fourth-grade student who has a profile of abilities similar to that of Alice. He does assignments well and on time, has high scores on national achievement tests and statewide mastery tests, and has impressed his teachers favorably every year. Yet Mrs. Rogers, his fourth-grade teacher, sees trouble ahead. When Mrs. Rogers assigned the class a creative writing task, Thomas handed in an assignment that, although a marvel of grammar and spelling, was basically a retelling of a story in the basal reader the class was using. Some of the other students whose grammar and spelling were not nearly as good were nevertheless much more imaginative in the stories they concocted. When Mrs. Rogers asked students to go out on a limb and draw their conception of a space alien and describe how it functioned, Thomas's drawing and description were quite decent but also quite human in character. Mrs. Rogers is concerned not about whether Thomas will do well in school but about whether he will find within himself the imagination to do well in and to enjoy life.

If schooling is preparation for the world of work, it is important to be concerned about whether schooling requires and develops creative thinking. Why? Because to compete in most jobs, Alice and Thomas will need to come up with their own ideas.

In science, for example, individuals need more than the ability to memorize facts in a book or to solve ready-made problems at the ends of chapters. The practice of science requires the ability to create significant ideas that make a difference to the field and, ultimately, to the world. People who generate important scientific ideas aren't necessarily those who are best at memorizing facts or solving textbook problems. Indeed, they may be people who don't particularly like to do these things and therefore don't show themselves at their best in school settings.

The same dynamic that applies in science applies in other occupations as well. Consider writing and art. It's one thing for individuals to succeed in writing good essays when they're told what to write about, or to draw nice pictures when they're told what pictures they should draw. It's quite another thing for individuals to come up with their own ideas for stories or pictures. For example, a bulletin board outside a classroom displays roughly two dozen pictures of children's houses. They are nice pictures of houses, but it is clear that the teacher told the students what to draw. It seems unlikely that two dozen children independently decided to draw pictures of their homes. In the real world of art and writing, artists and writers do not always have someone to give them a subject for their composition. Indeed, creative writers and artists are, almost by definition, people who come up with their own imaginative ideas. It is often unrealistic for teachers to formulate questions for students, because in real life students are required to formulate their own questions. Sometimes educators need to urge students to formulate problems for themselves rather than pose problems for them.

A person could argue that most students will not become scientists, artists, or writers, but the situation is no different when applied to a very pragmatic occupation such as business. Many executives interviewed during studies of practical intelligence (Sternberg et al., 2000) complained that if they hired a top-level graduate of a business school, they might get someone who was good at analyzing textbook cases but perhaps unable to come up with innovative ideas for new business products or services, packaging ideas that create more shelf space for a product, or ways to compete successfully with similar industries in other countries.

The point, of course, is that large gaps exist between the kind of performance needed for success in a business setting and the kind of performance needed for success in school, even a school that is supposed to be quite practical in training students for the world of business. Thus, educated adults are often unable to do what is expected of them.

The same problem afflicts the study of education itself. It's one thing to get A's in education courses and quite another to succeed when called upon to innovate in a classroom setting.

Experience shows just how challenging classroom situations can be. For example, many teachers have had instructional techniques that work marvelously one year, and then for whatever reason, bomb the next year. The students look more or less the same, and the technique is definitely the same. However, it just fails to connect with the new class in the same way that it connected with the previous class. The uncreative teacher may blame the students or simply be convinced that she has a good technique, and if the students are unable to benefit from it, that's their hard luck. The creative teacher, however, recognizes that teaching is never static. Teachers constantly need to expand their repertoire to meet the needs of new students. The creative teacher views the situation as an opportunity to be a lifelong learner and to devise and try something new, and thereby to benefit not only the students, but also herself.

Why is it that students considered bright tend to be bright like Alice and Thomas? In other words, why are they so often test-smart but not necessarily smart in other ways?

Is it possible that children are not born to be smart only in this limited way, but that they are shaped to be smart in this way? The U.S. system of education, in essence, creates "Alices" by continually reinforcing or rewarding students for being test-smart. Indeed, the main lesson students learn is that it pays to be smart like Alice. As rewards for learning this lesson, students receive good grades, placement in high tracks, awards, and admission to impressive universities.

One indication that schools mold students into Alices comes from a study of the Kpelle tribe in Africa (Cole, Gay, Glick, & Sharp, 1971). Glick asked adult members of the tribe to sort terms into categories. For example, they were asked to sort names of fruits (apple, orange, grapefruit), names of vegetables (celery, lettuce, broccoli), or names of vehicles (bus, boat, car). Glick found that the Kpelle sorted functionally. For example, they would sort *apple* with *eat* and *car* with *gas*, because people eat apples and cars use gas.

In the U.S. culture, only young children sort functionally. The Kpelle's functional sorting behavior is considered stupid when done by an adult in the United States. Older children and adults are expected to sort taxonomically (putting fruits together) or hierarchically (putting the word *fruit* over the names of different fruits and then perhaps putting the word *food* over the whole group).

Glick tried, without actually instructing the Kpelle on how to sort taxonomically, to get the Kpelle to sort other than functionally. When Glick was about to conclude that they simply did not have the mental ability to do things any differently, as a last resort he decided to ask them how a stupid person would do the task. At this point, with no trouble at all, they sorted taxonomically. Why would the Kpelle consider taxonomic sorting stupid? The answer is that the Kpelle did not grow up in the Western educational system and—even more important—did not take Western tests.

In everyday life, people tend to think functionally. They think of eating apples or using gas in their cars. They learn to think taxonomically in school, but for the most part this kind of thinking remains limited to artificial settings. A problem arises, therefore, when advanced students or career aspirants have to start thinking in ways they have not been conditioned in school to think, that is, when they need to start turning out their own ideas rather than recite or analyze ideas other people have had.

Because these kinds of skills often have not been actively encouraged or selected, students tend not to develop them. In this respect, then, U.S. schools essentially mislead and prepare students poorly by developing and rewarding a set of skills that, although important in later life, are much less so than they are in school.

Barbara, the Creative Thinker

Barbara exhibited a different way of being intelligent. Her grades were good but not great. Although her aptitude test scores were very weak, her undergraduate teachers thought she was terrific.

When Barbara applied to a graduate program in psychology, she was rejected by an almost unanimous vote. In fact, only one faculty member voted to admit her. Even though Barbara had included a portfolio of her work that demonstrated a high degree of competence, most of the admissions people decided largely on the basis of her aptitude test scores. In other words, they had more confidence in fallible and often weak predictors of creative work than they had in the work itself. This odd situation is often seen in current educational practices. The predictor of performance has become more important than the performance itself!

"Barbaras" do not occur only at the graduate level. My daughter, Sara, was a student in a public school comprised of largely middle-class students. Her elementary school teacher was doing a unit on the planets. To acquaint students with the planet Mars, the teacher asked the class to imagine themselves as astronauts. They were to dress up as astronauts and decide what they would do when they landed on Mars.

Sara raised her hand to make a suggestion: What if she dressed up as a Martian and greeted the astronauts when they arrived on Mars? The teacher immediately nixed Sara's idea, explaining that it was known from space probes that there are no residents on Mars; therefore, it would not be appropriate in the context of a science lesson for Sara to dress up as a Martian.

When I heard about this incident, I was quite distressed. The teacher was certainly within her rights to reply as she did. But how many times do students have creative ideas, state them, and immediately get punished for doing so? And what is the lesson they learn from this kind of experience? They probably learn that the next time they have a creative idea, they should keep it to themselves. Is this the lesson educators want students to learn?

However, the teacher's behavior was understandable and no doubt well intentioned. For one thing, there probably are no Martians (although, for a variety of reasons, that is not certain—they might live underground; they might be sending false feedback to space probes; they might be a life form the space probes cannot recognize, etc.). For another thing, the teacher, as all teachers, probably had a staggering amount of material she was trying to cover over the course of the term. It's easy for teachers to become concerned that diversions prevent complete coverage of material and that students will not get a fair shake when it comes to statewide examinations. Yet there are few teacher actions that kill creativity more effectively than discouraging creative ideas when they are proposed.

Why has Barbara's future been jeopardized, and why is Sara's at risk as well? Why do teachers, professors, school administrators, and corporate executives pay more attention to predictors than to performance?

And, in general, why do they pay so much attention to results on tests of IQ and related abilities? They do so because they are trapped in a closed system that works only to the advantage of a relatively small number of people, and not necessarily to the advantage of people who have the most potential to contribute to society.

Celia, the Practical Thinker

When Celia applied to a graduate program in psychology, she had test scores that were good but not great, grades that were good but not great, and letters of recommendation that were good but not great. In fact, just about everything in her application seemed to be good but not great. Naturally, Celia was admitted—every program needs people who are good but not great. Indeed, in this program, Celia's work proved to be pretty much what had been predicted: good but not great. So it seemed that, finally, an accurate prediction had been made—for once!

What a surprise Celia gave the school when it came to getting a job. Everyone wanted to hire Celia! That raised an intriguing question. Why would someone who lacked Alice's analytical ability and Barbara's creative ability do so well in the job market?

The answer is actually very simple. Celia was something like the second boy in the grizzly bear story. She had an abundance of practical intelligence, or simple common sense. She could go into an environment, figure out what she needed to do to thrive there, and then do it.

For example, Celia knew how to interview effectively, how to interact well with others, and how to get her work done. She also was aware of what kinds of things do and do not work. In other words, she was street-smart in an academic setting. She knew something that is seldom acknowledged: in school, as in life, an individual needs a certain amount of practical intelligence to adapt to the environment.

One kind of evidence for this intelligence comes from studies of students in diverse settings. For example, Carraher, Carraher, and Schliemann (1985; see also Ceci & Roazzi, 1994; Nuñes, 1994) did a study that is especially relevant for assessing intelligence as adaptation to the environment. They studied Brazilian street children. Brazilian street children are under great contextual pressure to form a successful street business. If they do not, they risk death at the hands of so-called death squads. These death squads murder children who, unable to earn money, resort to robbing stores (or those they suspect of robbing stores). The researchers found that the same children who were able to do the mathematics needed to run their street businesses were often minimally able or unable to do school mathematics. In fact, the more abstract and removed from real-world contexts the problems were in presentation, the worse the children did on the problems. These results suggest that differences in context can have a powerful effect on performance.

Such differences are not limited to Brazilian street children. Lave (1988) showed that Berkeley housewives who successfully did the mathematics needed for comparison shopping in the supermarket were unable to do the same mathematics when they were placed in a classroom and given isomorphic problems presented in an abstract form. In other words, the housewives' inability was not at the level of mental processes but at the level of applying the processes in specific environmental contexts.

In other research, both in the United States and in other countries, the authors found results consistent with those described. Some international studies are described because they call into question the straightforward interpretation of results from conventional tests of intelligence that suggest the existence of a general factor of intelligence.

In a study in Usenge, Kenya, near the city of Kisumu, the ability of school-age students to adapt to their indigenous environment was examined. A test of practical intelligence for adaptation to the environment was devised (see Sternberg, 2004; Sternberg & Grigorenko, 1997; Sternberg et al., 2001). The test measured a student's informal knowledge of natural herbal medicines that Usenge villagers believe can be used to fight various types of infections. At least some of these medicines appear to be effective (F. Okatcha, personal communication, 1998). Most villagers certainly believe in their efficacy, as shown by the fact that children in the villages use their knowledge of these medicines an average of once a week in medicating themselves and others. Thus, tests of how to use these medicines constitute effective measures of one aspect of practical intelligence as defined by the villagers as well as life circumstances in the village environmental context. Middle-class Westerners might find it quite a challenge to thrive or even survive in these contexts or, for that matter, in the context of urban ghettos not so distant from their comfortable homes.

The Kenyan children's ability to identify the medicines—where they come from, what they are used for, and how they are dosed—was measured. Based on work done elsewhere, scores on this test were expected not to correlate with scores on conventional tests of intelligence. To test this hypothesis, a variety of Western-style intelligence tests were also administered to the eighty-five students. In addition, the students were given a comparable test of vocabulary in their own Dholuo language. (The Dholuo language is spoken in the home, while English is spoken in the schools.)

Statistically significant correlations of the practical intelligence tests with the tests of verbal ability and achievement were found. The correlations, however, were negative. In other words, the higher the students scored on the tests of practical intelligence, the lower they scored, on average, on the tests of academic verbal skills, such as vocabulary and English grammar. This surprising result can be interpreted in various ways, but based on the ethnographic observations of the cultural anthropologists on the team, it was concluded that a plausible scenario takes into account the familial expectations for the students.

In this culture, students generally drop out of school before graduation, and most families in the village do not particularly value formal Western schooling. There is no reason why they should, as their children will, for the most part, spend their lives farming or engaged in other occupations that make little or no use of Western schooling. These families emphasize teaching students the indigenous informal knowledge that leads to successful adaptation in their environments. Students who spend their time learning the indigenous practical knowledge of the community generally do not invest themselves heavily in doing well in school; students who do well in school generally do not invest themselves as heavily in learning the indigenous knowledge—hence the negative correlations (Sternberg & Grigorenko, 1997; Sternberg et al., 2001).

The Kenya study suggests that the identification of a so-called general factor of human intelligence may tell more about how abilities interact with patterns of schooling—and especially Western patterns of schooling—than it does about the structure of human abilities. In Western schooling, students typically study a variety of subjects from an early age and thus develop skills in a variety of areas. This kind of schooling prepares students to take intelligence tests that typically measure skills in a variety of areas. Often intelligence tests measure skills that students were expected to acquire a few years before taking the intelligence tests. But as Rogoff (1990) and others have noted, this pattern of schooling is not universal and has not been common for much of the history of humankind. Throughout history and in many places still, schooling, especially for boys, takes the form of apprenticeships in which students learn a craft beginning at an early age. They learn what they will need to know to succeed in a trade, but not a lot more. They are not engaged simultaneously in tasks that require the development of the particular blend of skills measured by conventional intelligence tests.

Because students do not do well on conventional Western-style tests, they quickly begin to disassociate from them. This phenomenon is by no means limited to African villages. When studying African American college students in the United States, Steele and Aronson (1995) found that many of the students stopped caring about how they performed on ability and achievement tests because they had come to view these tests as irrelevant to their own image of themselves. Feeling hopeless about such tasks, they viewed them as irrelevant. The investigators found, however, that when they told the students that on a particular verbal test there was no difference in scores between African American and Anglo students, the African Americans' scores shot up. What is also interesting is that the Anglo students' scores went down. A similar phenomenon was demonstrated with respect to women in mathematics. Told that, on a given difficult mathematics test, no difference in scores was evident between men and women, women scored higher and men scored lower.

The results of this study capture many of the points made in this chapter. The tendency of teachers to mistakenly undervalue certain forms of intelligence can be costly. In a study in California, conceptions of intelligence among parents of children from different ethnic groups were compared (Okagaki & Sternberg, 1993). It was found that some parents—Anglo and Asian—gave greater emphasis to the importance of cognitive skills than to intelligence. Other parents, primarily Latino, emphasized the importance of social skills. When teachers were asked their conceptions of intelligence, they emphasized cognitive skills.

The study found that the more parents emphasized social competence skills in their conception of intelligence, such as getting along with peers and helping out the family, the less intelligent their children appeared according to the standards of the school (Okagaki & Sternberg, 1993). In other words, the mismatch between what the parents emphasized in their home environment and what the schools required in their environment resulted in students who might be quite competent in the home and community setting but were judged as intellectually lacking in school. The bottom line, then, is that one of the best ways to improve students' achievement is to value the skills they bring to bear on that achievement. If their skills are valued, these students are likely to experience higher achievement.

How can teachers value and develop the skills of various students? Methods teachers can use to value and develop the three thinking skills are discussed in Chapters 4, 5, and 6, and how teachers can structure and implement lessons for the classroom is presented in Chapters 7 and 8.

PART II

Building Successful Intelligence Abilities

Chapter 4:   Teaching for Analytical Thinking

Chapter 5:   Teaching for Creative Thinking

Chapter 6:   Teaching for Practical Thinking

It is important for the reader to take an active role in processing the material presented in this part of the book. To make the theory of successful intelligence work, each reader must generate personal, specific, situated examples. Moreover, it is important to generate examples in a variety of subject areas, applying the theory across a teacher's teaching spectrum and to all of a teacher's students.

Each lesson in the three chapters of this part of the book includes a brief introduction followed by a discussion of lesson content that helps teachers establish a particular thinking ability in students. A common format is used for each lesson. A targeted skill is identified, followed by a few *prompt words or phrases* that help engender and encourage the appropriate thinking skill. Some prompts are from the perspective of the teacher; others are from the perspective of the student. Next, the "Using It in Life" section shows examples of the skill from life outside the classroom. "Taking It to the Classroom" provides examples that apply the prompts to different grade levels in eight subject areas and are marked to show a suggested school level: P for primary grades, I for intermediate grades, HS for high school, and C for college. Finally, in "Taking It to Heart," readers are given the chance to use the prompts to create examples for their own teaching situations. Creating personalized examples is strongly encouraged, because this active involvement helps make the ideas personal and memorable.

Teaching For Analytical Thinking

The lessons in this chapter build the foundational skill of analytical thinking. The first six lessons introduce the individual steps in solving problems and serve as prompts for developing analytical skills. The seventh lesson provides additional prompts to promote analytical thinking.

PROBLEM SOLVING

Analytical intelligence, the first component of successful intelligence, involves the conscious direction of mental processes to find a thoughtful solution to a problem. Analytical thinking can be used for different purposes. In problem solving, the goal is to move from a problem situation (e.g., not having enough money to buy a car) to a solution, overcoming obstacles along the way. In decision making, the goal is to select from choices or to evaluate opportunities (e.g., choose the best car for the amount of money available). The two processes, although not completely the same, share many of the same analytical skills.

The problem-solving cycle refers to the set of processes people use to solve problems. The set comprises a cycle in that it repeats itself: today's solution becomes tomorrow's problem. If a person solves the current dissatisfaction with his or her car by buying another car, sooner or later, that new car—the solution to the old set of problems—presents a new set of problems. The order in which the steps are taken in this cycle is not fixed. People may change the order of the steps to reach a solution to a problem they face.

After decades of bickering, psychologists have reached a reasonable consensus as to the higher-order processes used in problem solving. The names of these processes may differ for different psychologists, but the processes do not. One version of this set of processes is shown in the box below (Sternberg, 1977, 1979, 1980a, 1980b, 1981b, 1985). This list of six skills is not exhaustive, nor are the skills mutually exclusive. However, the processes on the list represent what people do when they solve problems.

Six Skills in Problem Solving

1. Identify the problem

2. Allocate resources

3. Represent and organize information

4. Formulate a strategy

5. Monitor problem-solving strategies

6. Evaluate solutions

LESSON 1: IDENTIFY THE PROBLEM

Targeted skill: Identifying the problem

Prompt words or phrases: identify, figure out, recognize, name, define, detect, understand

In this step, a problem solver needs both to recognize that there is a problem and to define what the problem is. For example, a student is assigned to write a social studies paper on a topic of his or her choice. The quality of the outcome depends, in large part, on the topic chosen; some topics will not yield an interesting paper, regardless of what a student does with them. There may be little or no literature on a topic (e.g., "An Analysis of Laramie, Wyoming, in Prehistoric Times"), or the topic may be so broad that it does not lend itself to a sensible student paper (e.g., "Government").

The ability to identify problems is measured indirectly by ability tests, but in an academic way. Intelligence and other tests frequently include distractor answers that are the right answers to different (i.e., wrong) problems. On arithmetic problem-solving tests, distractors are often correct answers to smaller parts of the full problem and thus might be correct outcomes for intermediate stages of a problem solution. The idea, quite bluntly, is to trick test takers into thinking that one of the incorrect answers is correct, when in fact it is only a partial solution to the problem. For example, Alice (mentioned in Chapter 3) may be quite adept at solving problems, but she is not necessarily adept at identifying good problems to solve. She does well on essay tests if she is given a topic on which to write, but not so well if she has to generate the topic herself.

Using It in Life

The ability to define problems properly is of key importance in everyday, not just academic, settings. In 1974, Detroit car manufacturers suffered severe financial damage when they thought the royal road to profits was making larger and larger and more and more expensive cars. The gas crunch hit and people turned to smaller cars, which Japanese manufacturers had ready for U.S. consumers. Since then the desire for small or large cars has cycled back and forth. The key is for a manufacturer to identify the coming need before another manufacturer does.

Another example from the automobile industry involves Japan as well. U.S. automobile manufacturers complained for years about being excluded from Japanese markets and blamed the Japanese government for their exclusion. In the past, their cars had been failures in the Japanese marketplace, but it was disingenuous for the manufacturers to place the blame on the Japanese government. In Japan, people drive on the left side of the road, as in England. Yet Detroit had been attempting to sell cars with the driver's cockpit (steering wheel, brakes, gas pedal, etc.) on the left side of the car. It's little wonder that

Japanese consumers were not interested in U.S. cars. Japanese manufacturers, in contrast, have never tried to sell cars with the driver's gear on the right side in the United States. U.S. manufacturers identified the problem as trade restrictions, when in fact a much more accurate definition of the problem was the desirability of their cars for a particular market. In the new millennium, ironically, so many automobile manufacturers are multinational that it is sometimes difficult to ascertain who is competing with whom!

Politicians are notorious for misidentifying problems. In 1972, the Nixon administration made a big mistake, and then made an even bigger one. The big mistake was sending men to burglarize the office of the Democratic National Committee in the Watergate Hotel for reasons that are still uncertain. The burglars had the misfortune to be caught, resulting in an enormous scandal.

But the second, and much bigger, mistake for the administration was to institute a massive cover-up, which proved disastrous. As the cover-up unraveled, there was plenty of bad news to give the people, but it was given painfully slowly, in bits: this tactic exactly counters the advice of Machiavelli, who warned that if there is good news to give the people, dribble it out slowly, but if there is bad news, give it to them all at once. In misidentifying the problem as one of covering up rather than coming clean, the Nixon administration lost everything. Participants were tried and convicted, and Nixon himself eventually resigned his office. Obviously, such cover-ups are not limited to Republicans, as the disastrous Monica Lewinsky affair in the Clinton administration proved.

Businesses can have the same quandary with misidentification of a problem. The A. H. Robins Company tried to hide from the public the enormous injury to women done by an intrauterine device (the Dalkon Shield) they produced. As a result, after the extent of the damage became public in spite of their cover-up attempts, the company was forced into bankruptcy. In contrast, when someone laced Extra Strength Tylenol with cyanide, Johnson & Johnson immediately publicized the problem and recalled all of the product from the market. In the short run, they lost money. However, in the long run, the company gained, and the product quickly recovered its status as the leading pain reliever.

Another company also discovered the results of misinterpreting a problem. Intel found that when they tried to make light of a flaw in a Pentium microchip, huge amounts of bad publicity resulted. As soon as they admitted the error existed and offered free replacements, the general public lost interest in the problem.

Taking It to the Classroom

The goal of teaching for analytical skills is to encourage students to formulate and ask questions, not just to answer them. Thus, teachers should encourage students to pose what they see as fundamental questions about whatever topic they are studying. In class discussions or individual conferences, students should also be encouraged to think about why these questions are important.

Language arts (I): Teachers can encourage students to select a book on which to write a report.

Mathematics (P–C): Teachers can encourage students to recognize what a math problem is really asking.

Science (I–C): Teachers can encourage students to define a question for a science project.

Social studies (I–C): Teachers can encourage students to identify a topic for a history paper.

Foreign language (HS–C): Teachers can encourage students to figure out an effective way to learn a list of foreign language equivalents to an English word.

Art (P–I): Teachers can encourage students to choose a scene to sketch.

Music (P): Teachers can encourage students to pick a song to sing.

Physical education (I–HS): Teachers can encourage students to detect why they keep dropping the baseball when it is thrown to them.

Taking It to Heart

Teachers should list five activities they can assign and discuss with students that will help them understand and identify problems.

LESSON 2: ALLOCATE RESOURCES

Targeted skill: Allocating resources

Prompt words or phrases: allocate, allot, set apart, divide, share, trade off

In this step, a problem solver decides how much time, effort, and other resources (such as money or personnel) to allocate to the solution of a problem. For virtually all tasks, only a limited amount of time and other resources can be allocated for the entire project. At this initial phase, it is important to partition those available resources into chunks for each subtask in the project.

Poor resource allocation may turn a potentially excellent product into a mediocre one. For example, students commonly do not allow sufficient time for the actual writing of a paper. They may spend a great deal of the available time researching, then find that if they had set aside more time for writing, they could have written a much better paper. As a result, the final product does not accurately represent the work that went into it.

In one study, Wagner and Sternberg (1987) considered people's time allocation when they read. They noticed what appeared to be a flaw in the kinds of tests used to measure reading comprehension. Such tests seemed to give a relatively incomplete view of what it means to be a good reader.

When taking a reading test, students read all passages for maximum comprehension, because they know that the tester can and probably will ask almost anything about the passage they have read. Following each passage, there are usually both general and detailed questions. In real life, whether in school, on the job, or when reading for pleasure, people do not read for maximum comprehension. Their reading purpose influences their reading strategy. As they read a newspaper or a magazine in real life, people rarely attend to details, whereas if they read instructions on how to put together a piece of equipment, they pay great attention to the details.

As students, good readers should allocate time as a function of how they will be tested. For example, they may read a history assignment differently depending on whether they will be tested through writing a general essay or with a detailed multiple-choice test.

In the Wagner and Sternberg (1987) study, participants read different kinds of reading passages with different purposes in mind: for the main ideas, for the gist of the passage, for details, and for analysis and evaluation. How the participants allocated their time was examined. Good readers allocated their time differently, depending upon the purpose for which they were reading a given passage. Average and poor readers, however, either showed no differential time allocation across types of passages or showed arbitrary time allocation. Their systems did not correspond to the assignments they were given. In short, time allocation is a crucial part of good reading but is not fully measured by reading tests.

Using It in Life

Time allocation is also important on the job. President Jimmy Carter was notorious for his inability or unwillingness to allocate his time effectively. He seemed unable or unwilling to delegate authority adequately and thus ended up attending to trivia that would have been best left to subordinates. At the same time, higher-level decision making was often delayed or insufficiently considered, as in the stunning failure of the rescue mission of U.S. citizens trapped in Iran.

Other presidents have gone almost to the opposite extreme. For example, Ronald Reagan was known for delegating almost everything and got into trouble because some of the people to whom he delegated tasks did not do the tasks as scrupulously as the public might have hoped. Bill Clinton seemed to maintain a more balanced strategy than some of his predecessors, delegating or not delegating according to the priority of the task. President George W. Bush seems to have delegated authority, but resignations such as that former Defense Secretary Rumsfeld show the importance of being careful in choosing those to whom one delegates authority.

Taking It to the Classroom

The goal is for teachers to help students decide what resources they need to complete a task. Therefore, instead of telling them what resources to use or how much time to take, teachers should ask students and let them decide how to allocate resources to a task. The teacher can then determine whether the allocation of resources makes sense, given the problem.

Language arts (HS–C): Teachers can encourage students to decide how much time to spend studying for an English test.

Mathematics (I–C): Teachers can ask students to divide their time between parts of a test that seems too long to complete in the test period.

Science (I–C): Teachers can ask students to allot time to complete a lab project.

Social studies (HS–C): Teachers can prompt students to decide how many resources to use in a debate on whether the UN should have intervened to a greater extent in West Darfur, where genocide has been occurring.

Foreign language (I–C): Teachers can ask students to decide how much time to allocate for memorizing a list of words.

Art (P–HS): Teachers can encourage students to select appropriate colors of paint for a still life from those available.

Music (P–I): Teachers can ask students to decide in which key or at what tempo to sing a song.

Physical education (I–C): Teachers can request that students allocate energy between working out and basketball practice.

Taking It to Heart

Teachers should list five activities they can assign and discuss with students that will help them understand and use the process of allocation of resources.

LESSON 3: REPRESENT AND ORGANIZE INFORMATION

Targeted skill: Representing and organizing information

Prompt words or phrases: order, sequence, represent, denote, portray, arrange, organize

In this step, problem solvers need to represent and organize information in an understandable and useful way. A student collecting information for a paper on the United States as the world's police officer might organize his or her notes by authors of books and articles, by titles of books or articles, by topics to include in the paper, or in any number of ways. How the information is organized may determine how effectively the paper can be written.

I quickly learned the value of organization during a move from one office to another. In a hurry to get ready for teaching, I placed all my books on long rows of bookshelves in essentially random order. In this way, I saved the time it would have taken to arrange the books in a systematic way, such as alphabetically by author. But I paid dearly for this haphazard storage: Whenever I needed a book, I had to go through hundreds of books to find it. Eventually, I was compelled to arrange the books so I could access them efficiently.

This example shows a general principle of expertise in problem solving. Expert problem solvers devote more time early in the problem-solving cycle to represent and organize information so that they can spend less time solving the problem later (Sternberg, 1981a, 1999).

Using It in Life

Representation and organization of information are important in many life pursuits—for example, negotiations of any kind. Some Israelis view certain Palestinian leaders as murderers and liars whose words cannot be trusted in the slightest. Of course, some Palestinians regard certain Israeli leaders in the same way. As long as opponents are represented as basically dishonest and distrust exists, meaningful negotiations are just about impossible.

As another example, since 1998, after carrying out nuclear detonations in close succession, both India and Pakistan have been regularly testing missiles. After each of such tests, the newspapers in these rival countries have published statements about their national pride in their defense capability and its reliability as a deterrent to nuclear war (see, e.g., Associated Press, 2007, written after a nuclear-capable missile test in Pakistan). Yet newspapers in each country have portrayed the government of the other country as run by liars and scoundrels. Such reports may serve the politicians' short-term purposes in fanning supposed patriotism, but as long as each side totally disbelieves in the credibility of the other, meaningful negotiations are unattainable.

Misrepresentation of information perhaps reaches its extreme in neurologically impaired patients, as shown in this example:

There was a hint of a smile on his face. He also appeared to have decided that the examination was over and started to look around for his hat. He reached out his hand and took hold of his wife's head, tried to lift it off, and put it on. He had apparently mistaken his wife for a hat! His wife looked as if she was used to such things. (Sacks, 1985, p. 11)

Taking It to the Classroom

Often, students are asked simply to solve math problems, write papers, or read books. Teachers can help students organize their thinking by requesting them to show their work in math problems, provide outlines or concept maps for papers, or create character studies. Teachers can then comment to the students on the quality of their organization in problem solving.

Language arts (I–C): Teachers can encourage students to arrange topics in writing a paper.

Mathematics (I–C): Teachers can request that students represent verbal information with an equation in a math problem.

Science (HS–C): Teachers can ask students to draw a diagram that represents forces acting on a moving body.

Social studies (C): Teachers can encourage students to contrast U.S. versus Japanese representations of concepts in language (alphabetically versus pictographically).

Foreign language (I–C): Teachers can request that students use images (pictures in the mind) to help link foreign words with English words (e.g., imagine a person wearing a colorful shirt when learning the Spanish word *camisa* for *shirt*).

Art (P–HS): Teachers can ask students to depict various elements of a scene on a canvas.

Music (I–C): Teachers can ask students to examine the difference between the usual representation of music via an eight-tone musical scale and a representation via a twelve-tone scale.

Physical education (P–I): Teachers can encourage students to learn how the players in the field are organized in the game of baseball (e.g., first base, second base, etc.).

Taking It to Heart

Teachers should list five activities they can assign and discuss with students that will help them understand and use the process of representation and organization of information.

LESSON 4: FORMULATE A STRATEGY

Targeted skill: Formulating a strategy

Prompt words or phrases: strategize, plan, lay out, plot, contrive, concoct, draw up, sort

Selection and representation of information must be accompanied by the formulation of a strategy for sequencing processes in the order in which a problem solver will act on the representation. Ineffective sequencing of steps can result in not only wasted time and effort but also a poor product. For example, a student might try to write the introduction to a paper before completing the research, thinking that although the research might affect the main body of the paper, it should have little or no effect on a section that merely describes the goals and motivations behind the paper. But as experienced authors know, goals and motivations often change as a project progresses, and sometimes the final paper is not anything like the paper the author originally intended to write.

Using It in Life

Strategy formation is a key part of intelligence, a fact illustrated by the O. J. Simpson criminal trial. The defense team chose to rely heavily on a jury selection consultant, who helped them decide which potential jurors would be likely to arrive at a not-guilty verdict. The prosecution hired a jury consultant but chose not to rely on the advice given, even though the consultant viewed the jury that was selected as heavily in favor of the defense. It is now a matter of history that the defense strategy was successful, whereas the strategy of the prosecution was disastrous for their goal.

Strategy formation in business plays a large part in determining whether a business succeeds or fails. From their beginnings, IBM and Apple formulated completely different strategies for maximizing profits from their operating systems. IBM opted for an open system that others could and did copy. Although this strategy encouraged clones, it also resulted in enormous amounts of software being created for IBM and IBM-compatible computers. IBM's fortune became tied to the success of its marketing finesse, which was not always, perhaps, the greatest. Apple, on the other hand, decided to create a proprietary operating system and zealously guarded its rights to it. As a result, relatively little software was created for Apple's system, and its market share declined. Only with the introduction of the iMac computer and the iPod has Apple started to recover from this misguided strategy.

These examples, as well as the following example, demonstrate that bad strategy formulation can be costly. A trader in the United States for the Daiwa Bank of Japan made some bad decisions regarding investments and lost $400,000. He decided that he needed to rethink his strategies to gain back the money. Possibly in collusion with high officials of the bank, he hid his bad trades and tried to recoup his losses. He never did recover the losses and was ultimately discovered, but not before the bank's losses reached into the billions of dollars. This was definitely a bad strategy on the trader's part, not to mention the bank's.

Taking It to the Classroom

The main idea is for teachers to encourage students to plan their problem solving before jumping into it—to be reflective rather than impulsive problem solvers. Teachers should encourage students, therefore, to discuss strategies with the class before they begin to solve problems. They can also have students solicit feedback from other students on the strengths and weaknesses of their strategies.

Language arts (HS–C): Teachers can have students decide how to read two novels when comprehension will be tested for one novel by a detailed multiple-choice test and for the other by a two-page book report.

Mathematics (I–C): Teachers can ask students to figure out the order that mathematical operations should be applied in order to solve an equation (e.g., $[3x + 2] / 8 = 26$).

Science (P–C): Teachers can prompt students to order the steps in an experiment.

Social studies (I–C): Teachers can encourage students to plan what sources to consult initially and what sources to consult later when writing a history paper.

Foreign language (I–C): Teachers can prompt students to judge which words to give priority to on a vocabulary test when there are too many words in a unit for them to learn all of them.

Art (P–I): Teachers can request that students lay out the order in which the parts of a human body should be drawn in a sketch.

Music (P–C): Teachers can ask students to contrive a strategy for learning to play a difficult piano piece for a recital.

Physical education (P–C): Teachers can encourage students to devise a strategy for defeating an opponent in tennis (e.g., hit many shots to the opponent's backhand if the opponent is weak in returning such shots).

Taking It to Heart

Teachers should list five activities they can assign and discuss with students that will help them understand and use the process of strategy formulation.

LESSON 5: MONITOR PROBLEM-SOLVING STRATEGIES

Targeted skill: Monitoring strategies

Prompt words or phrases: check, review, monitor, oversee, reflect, inspect, audit, make sure

As individuals proceed through a problem-solving task, they must track what they have already done, be aware of what they are currently doing, and check on what remains to be done. They must also verify that their strategies for solving the problem are bringing them closer to solutions. Monitoring, then, is the ongoing activity during problem solving that ensures that the problem solving is going the desired way. In writing a research paper, for example, it is important to track sources consulted so as not to waste time consulting them again. Furthermore, individuals need to track what information has been collected and what information still needs to be collected.

Using It in Life

Lapses in monitoring strategies are responsible for some of the more grievous failures people encounter in their personal lives. In studying personal relationships, for example, Sternberg (1998) was struck by the number of people who reported that they realized that what they now found to be intolerable flaws in their partners were not hidden from them before they decided to tie the knot. On the contrary, their partner's flaws were often quite noticeable, and third parties may have pointed them out. The evidence was there, but the individual chose not to see or tackle it. In other words, these individuals failed to adequately monitor their ongoing relationships.

Monitoring failures are costly at an organizational level as well. For example, the Central Intelligence Agency of the United States specializes in revealing and monitoring information, including well-hidden information. This fact makes all the more awesome the agency's failure to provide comprehensive information on the status of the production of weapons of mass destruction in Iraq in 2002. By the time such a comprehensive report was concluded in 2004, stating that at the time of the U.S. invasion in March 2003, Saddam Hussein did not possess stockpiles of illicit weapons and had not begun any program to produce them, the United States had already entered Iraq.

Taking It to the Classroom

Often students hand in only their final work. Teachers can encourage monitoring by having students hand in successive drafts of reports and essays and giving them feedback for each draft. Teachers should also encourage students to provide their own feedback regarding how they can improve their work.

Language arts (P–C): Teachers can ask students to determine whether the main points of a book are clear as they read it.

Mathematics (HS): Teachers can tell students to review steps in a geometric proof for evidence that they are moving toward the desired solution.

Science (HS–C): Teachers can encourage students to make sure that safety procedures are followed in a lab exercise in a chemistry course.

Social studies (I–C): Teachers can ask students to monitor progress in ongoing peace negotiations in some part of the world.

Foreign language (I–C): Teachers can prompt students to make sure they clearly understand the basic grammatical structures they need to know to advance in studying a language.

Art (P–I): Teachers can prompt students to compare whether a portrait in progress looks like its subject.

Music (HS): Teachers can tell students to determine whether a violin is being played in tune.

Physical education (P–HS): Teachers can ask students to ascertain whether a strategy against an opponent is working.

Taking It to Heart

Teachers should list five activities they can assign and discuss with students that will help them understand and use the process of monitoring problem-solving strategies.

LESSON 6: EVALUATE SOLUTIONS

Targeted skill: Evaluating solutions

Prompt words or phrases: evaluate, test, judge the worth of, review, edit, revise

This step involves the critical analysis of a problem solution that one has reached. Is it the right solution? In cases where there is no one correct answer, is it a good solution? This step may require sensitivity to feedback and the ability to translate feedback received into an action plan. In performing a task, there are often various sources of internal and external feedback. Internal feedback is derived from an individual's own perceptions of how well task performance has been accomplished, whereas external feedback is based on other people's perceptions. Sensitivity to feedback is a major determiner of a person's potential to improve his or her work. This ability is probably at least as relevant for future as for present task performance and problem solving.

Using It in Life

Many educational systems would improve immediately and substantially if evaluation was taken more seriously in schools. Relatively few of the programs schools implement are ever seriously evaluated; the large majority receives no formal evaluation at all (Sternberg & Bhana, 1986). Today, many school reform efforts are being made, but if the past is any key, few of them will be evaluated adequately.

Evaluation is also important in an individual's personal life, of course. People are often reluctant to evaluate actions when their personal interests may be threatened. For example, many people stay in failing relationships for long periods of time. After these relationships end, the people often report that during the relationship they were reluctant to seriously evaluate how the relationship was going because they found the evaluation too threatening. They state that they may have thought about the issue at times, but quickly dropped it because it was too painful to examine further. They conclude that had they seriously evaluated the relationship earlier, they might have left a long time before they did.

Evaluation is important at the national and international levels as well. For example, for many years the United States has had a policy of economic embargo against and political confrontation with Cuba. The goal, as originally stated, was to bring down the Castro government. Whatever goal this policy may have served, it has definitely not brought down the government. There are relatively few signs that the U.S. policy, whether it is or is not the correct one, has been seriously evaluated in terms of its original goal.

Taking It to the Classroom

Teachers can encourage evaluation by explicitly asking students to comment on the strengths and weaknesses of their own work and that of others. Teachers should emphasize the importance of constructive critique.

Language arts (P–C): Teachers can ask students to proofread a paper.

Mathematics (P–HS): Teachers can tell students to compare the answer to a math problem with common sense (e.g., one cannot hand a customer "negative" change).

Science (P–C): Teachers can prompt students to compare the actual results of an experiment to those that were predicted.

Social studies (HS–C): Teachers can have students review whether the persuasive arguments in a term paper can be refuted easily by someone with an opposing point of view.

Foreign language (P–HS): Teachers can ask students to test themselves on the vocabulary words they studied before an exam.

Art (I): Teachers can prompt students to evaluate whether a collage is aesthetically pleasing.

Music (P–HS): Teachers can encourage students to ask others for feedback about their performances after singing solos.

Physical education (HS–C): Teachers can have students evaluate why they lost a wrestling match.

Taking It to Heart

Teachers should list five activities they can assign and discuss with students that will help them understand and use the process of evaluation of a problem solution.

LESSON 7: ADDITIONAL PROMPTS FOR ANALYTICAL THINKING

Targeted skill: Thinking analytically

Prompt words or phrases: analyze, evaluate, compare and contrast, judge, critique, assess

This lesson provides several general prompts for teaching for analytical thinking. These prompts promote the integration of the steps in the problem-solving cycle and present students with problems that require use of all the steps.

Language Arts

- Teachers can ask students to analyze the main lesson to be learned from a proverb, such as, "A stitch in time saves nine."
- Teachers can have students evaluate what Scarlett O'Hara meant when she said, "Tomorrow is another day."
- Teachers can encourage students to compare and contrast the personalities of David Copperfield and Oliver Twist.
- Teachers can ask students how Tom Sawyer convinced his friends to whitewash a fence, and whether the way he convinced his friends is a technique we should use in our own lives.

Mathematics

- Teachers can ask students how addition and subtraction are similar.
- Teachers can request that students analyze the following word problem to determine the formula to use in solving it: If a train travels for five hours at a rate of seventy-five miles per hour, how far will it go?
- Teachers can ask students to assess the validity of a geometric proof.
- Teachers can tell students to compare and contrast base ten and base twelve arithmetic.

Science

- Teachers can encourage students to analyze data from an experiment to determine what it means scientifically.
- Teachers can have students evaluate whether an experiment really tests the hypothesis it is supposed to test.
- Teachers can request that students critique the heliocentric and geocentric theories of the universe, showing how they are similar and different.
- Teachers can ask students why the moon is not as bright as the sun.

Social Studies

- Teachers can ask students to analyze the effects of slavery that led to the Civil War.
- Teachers can request that students assess Harry Truman's decision to drop an atomic bomb on Nagasaki.
- Teachers can tell students to compare and contrast the American Revolution and the French Revolution.
- Teachers can ask students why the Founding Fathers decided to rebel against the rule of Great Britain.

Foreign Language

- Teachers can ask students to analyze the grammatical structure of a sentence.
- Teachers can help students evaluate the following sentence and then correct the grammatical error: *C'est le vie.*
- Teachers can ask students to compare and contrast *ser* and *estar* (the two forms of "to be" in Spanish).
- Teachers can ask students how one could become friends with another child who does not speak one's language.

Art

- Teachers can request that students analyze how Rembrandt achieved vivid effects with light (e.g., the effect that makes the light look as though it is actually coming through his paintings).
- Teachers can ask students to evaluate the style of Roy Lichtenstein, commenting on how someone could become famous as a serious artist for drawing cartoon characters.
- Teachers can have students compare and contrast the artistic styles of Seurat and Renoir.
- Teachers can ask students why great artists are more likely to use paints than crayons to draw their works of art.

Music

- Teachers can encourage students to analyze why Mozart achieved immortality as a great composer and Salieri did not.
- Teachers can ask students to judge how music might facilitate or interfere with someone's efforts to concentrate while studying.
- Teachers can request that students critique classical and rock music, commenting on similarities and differences.
- Teachers can ask students to listen to music in major and minor keys and then analyze what sounds different about the two kinds of music.

Physical Education

- Teachers can tell students to analyze the movements they need to execute a successful serve in tennis.
- Teachers can have students compare and contrast the strengths and weaknesses of an opposing soccer team.
- Teachers can ask students to critique the playing styles of a great tennis player, commenting on similarities and differences.
- Teachers can ask students why good sportsmanship is important.

Taking It to Heart

Teachers should write down five examples of how to use these general analytical prompts in their teaching.

Teaching For Creative Thinking

A politician and his wife decide to eat dinner in a fancy French restaurant in Washington, DC. The waiter approaches their table and asks the wife what she would like as an appetizer. "The pâté de foie gras," she tells the waiter. "And the main course?" the waiter asks. "The filet mignon," responds the politician's wife. "And the vegetable?" asks the waiter. "He'll have the same," responds the politician's wife.

This story makes three points. First, although politicians may not be very creative, at least their spouses are. Second, creativity is not an attribute limited to the greats—the Darwins, the Picassos, the Hemingways—it is something anyone can display. Third, creativity is a decision. The politician's wife decided, through her cutting remark, for creativity.

Creativity is a decision. People who are creative are like good investors: they buy low and sell high in the world of ideas. In this chapter, the idea of creativity as a decision—the investment theory of creativity—is described. Lessons are presented that include twelve techniques teachers can use to foster creativity in their students and themselves.

THE INVESTMENT VIEW OF CREATIVITY: BUYING LOW AND SELLING HIGH

The investment theory of creativity (Sternberg & Lubart, 1995a, 1995b) asserts that creative thinkers are like good investors: they buy low and sell high. Whereas investors do this in the world of finance, creative people do it in the world of ideas. Creative people generate ideas that are like undervalued stocks (i.e., stocks with a low price-to-earnings ratio), and generally both the ideas and the stocks are rejected by the public. When creative ideas are proposed, they are often viewed as bizarre, useless, or even foolish and summarily rejected. The person proposing them is often regarded with suspicion and perhaps even with disdain and derision.

Creative ideas are both novel and valuable. Why, then, are they rejected? Because the creative innovator challenges vested interests and defies the crowd. The crowd does not maliciously or willfully reject creative notions; rather, it does not realize and often does not want to realize that the proposed ideas often represent a valid and superior way of thinking. The crowd generally perceives opposition to the status quo as annoying, offensive, and reason enough to ignore innovative ideas.

Evidence abounds that creative ideas are often rejected (Sternberg & Lubart, 1995a). Initial reviews of major works of literature and art are frequently negative. Toni Morrison's (1982) *Tar Baby* received negative reviews when it was first published, as did Sylvia Plath's *The Bell Jar* (Lucas, 1963). The first exhibition in Munich of the Norwegian painter Edvard Munch opened and closed the same day because it received a strong negative response from the critics. Some of the greatest scientific papers are rejected by not just one but several journals before being published. John Garcia, a distinguished biopsychologist, was denounced summarily when he first proposed that a form of learning called classical conditioning could be produced in a single trial of learning (Garcia & Koelling, 1966).

From the investment view, then, the creative person buys low by presenting a unique idea. This individual then attempts to convince others of its value. If successful, this increases the perceived value of the investment, and the creative person sells high by leaving the idea to others and moving on to another. Although people typically want others to love their ideas, immediate universal applause for an idea usually indicates that it is not particularly creative.

Creativity is fostered by buying low and selling high in the world of ideas—by defying the crowd. Creativity is as much a decision about and an attitude toward life as it is a matter of ability. Creativity is witnessed routinely in young children but hard to find in older children and adults, because their creative potential has been suppressed by a society that encourages intellectual conformity. Children's natural creativity begins to be suppressed when they are expected to color within the lines in their coloring books. In essence, caregivers and teachers decide for children—and they decide to discourage natural creativity.

BALANCING ANALYTICAL,
CREATIVE, AND PRACTICAL ABILITIES

Creative work requires applying and balancing the three thinking abilities discussed in this book (Sternberg, 1985; Sternberg & Lubart, 1995a; Sternberg & O'Hara, 1999; Sternberg & Williams, 1996).

Analytical ability is typically considered to be critical thinking ability. A person with this skill analyzes and evaluates ideas. Everyone, even the most creative person, has better and worse ideas. Without well-developed analytical ability, the creative thinker is as likely to pursue bad ideas as good ones. The creative individual uses analytical ability both to work out the implications of a creative idea and to test it.

Creative ability is what is typically thought of as creativity. It is the ability to generate novel and interesting ideas. Often, the individual considered creative is a particularly good synthetic thinker who makes connections between things other people don't recognize spontaneously.

Practical ability is the ability to translate theory into practice and abstract ideas into practical accomplishments. An implication of the investment theory of creativity is that good ideas don't sell themselves. The creative person uses practical ability to convince other people that an idea is worthy. For example, every organization has a set of ideas that dictate how things, or at least some things, should be done. A new procedure must be sold by convincing others that it is better than the old one. Practical ability is also used to recognize ideas that have a potential audience.

Full creativity requires a balance among analytical, creative, and practical abilities. The person who is creative only in thinking may come up with innovative ideas, but she can't recognize or sell them. The person who is only analytical may be an excellent critic of other people's ideas, but he is unlikely to generate creative ideas. The person who is only practical may be an excellent salesperson, but she is as likely to sell ideas or products of little or no value as she is to sell those ideas with genuine worth.

Teachers should encourage and develop creativity by teaching students to find a balance among analytical, creative, and practical thinking. A creative attitude is at least as important as creative thinking skills are (Schank, 1988). Most teachers want to encourage creativity in their students, but they are not sure how to do so. Following are twelve strategies (see box below) that develop creativity (Sternberg & Lubart, 1995a; also see Sternberg & Williams, 1996). These strategies, though not independent of each other, are presented in discrete lessons. The strategies are presented in terms of teachers and students, but they apply equally to administrators working with teachers, parents working with children, and people trying to develop their own creativity.

Strategies for Creative Thinking

- Redefine the problem
- Question and analyze assumptions
- Sell creative ideas
- Generate ideas
- Recognize the two faces of knowledge
- Identify and surmount obstacles
- Take sensible risks
- Tolerate ambiguity
- Build self-efficacy
- Uncover true interests
- Delay gratification
- Model creativity

LESSON 8: REDEFINE THE PROBLEM

Targeted skill: Redefining problems

Prompt words or phrases: redefine, rephrase, change view, reframe, review

Redefining a problem means taking a problem and turning it on its head. Many times people have a problem and can't see how to solve it; they feel stuck in a box. Redefining a problem essentially means extricating oneself from the box.

Using It in Life

A good example of redefining a problem is represented through a story told by the wife of an executive at one of the Big Three automobile companies in the Detroit area. At the time she told the story, her husband was in a high-level position. He loved his job and the money he made, but he hated the person he worked for. He decided to find himself a new job, as he was unable to stand his boss any longer. He went to a headhunter, who assured him that a new job could easily be arranged. Then the executive talked to his wife, who was teaching a unit on redefining problems as part of a course she was teaching on applied intelligence (Sternberg, 1986; Sternberg, Kaufman, & Grigorenko, 2007). The executive realized that he could apply what she was teaching to his own problem. He returned to the headhunter and gave the headhunter his boss's name. The headhunter found a new job for the boss, which the boss—having no idea what was going on—accepted. The executive then got his boss's job. The executive decided for creativity—in this case, by redefining a problem.

Taking It to the Classroom

There are many ways teachers can encourage students to define and redefine problems for themselves, rather than doing it for them. Creative performance is promoted when students are encouraged to define and redefine their own problems and projects. Teachers can encourage creative thinking by having students select their own topics for papers or presentations, choose their own ways of solving problems, and rechoose if they discover that their selections were mistakes. Students should be allowed to pick their own topics, subject to review, on at least one paper each term. Reviewing the topic ensures that it is relevant to the lesson and has a chance of leading to a successful project. Teachers can use an initial bad choice to identify for students what makes a successful project. A successful project (a) is appropriate to the course's goals, (b) illustrates a student's mastery of at least some of what has been taught, and (c) can earn a good grade. If a topic is so far from the goals that it has a good chance of receiving a low grade, the teacher may prompt the student to choose another topic.

Teachers cannot always offer students choices, but making choices is the only way for them to learn how to choose. A real choice is not deciding between drawing a cat or a dog, nor is it picking one state in the United States to present at a project fair. Students need latitude in making choices to help them develop taste and good judgment, both of which are essential elements of creativity.

Everyone, at one time or another, makes mistakes in choosing a project or in selecting how to accomplish it. Teachers need to remind students that an important part of creativity is the analytical part, which includes learning to recognize that a mistake has been made. Students need to be given the opportunity to make mistakes and then be taught how to fix them.

Language arts (I–C): Teachers can ask students to rewrite a published story from the point of view of a character other than the narrator.

Mathematics (P–HS): Teachers can encourage students to find a different question to ask about an existing math problem.

Science (C): Teachers can prompt students to consider how a scientist working with a different paradigm from that of an experimenter would interpret the experimenter's results.

Social studies (P–I): Teachers can ask students to compare how greetings in one culture differ from those in another.

Foreign language (HS–C): Teachers can request that students consider how grammar causes communication to be structured differently in English from how it is structured in another language.

Art (P–HS): Teachers can encourage students to represent an object in two entirely different media.

Music (P–I): Teachers can have students sing two different melodies using the same words or sing the same melody using two different sets of words.

Physical education (P–C): Teachers can ask students to play the same game with two different sets of rules, such as baseball with two different distances between bases.

Taking It to Heart

Teachers should give five examples of how to help students practice redefining problems.

LESSON 9: QUESTION AND ANALYZE ASSUMPTIONS

Targeted skill: Questioning and analyzing assumptions

Prompt words or phrases: what if, assume, question, doubt

Everyone assumes. Often, a person does not know that he or she is assuming because his or her assumptions are widely shared. Creative people question these assumptions and eventually lead others to question them as well. Questioning assumptions is part of the analytical thinking involved in creativity.

Using It in Life

When Copernicus suggested that the earth revolves around the sun, the suggestion was viewed as preposterous because everyone could see that the sun revolved around the earth. Galileo's ideas, including the relative rates of falling objects, caused him to be banned as a heretic. When an individual questions the way a department functions, the head of the department often does not smile. These examples represent individuals who question assumptions that are simply accepted—assumptions that many do not wish to question. Sometimes it is not until many years later that the crowd realizes the limitations or errors of their assumptions and the value of the creative person's thoughts. The impetus of those who question assumptions allows for cultural, technological, and other forms of advancement.

Taking It to the Classroom

Teachers can be role models for questioning assumptions by showing students that what they assume they know, they may not really know.

Of course, students should not question every assumption. There are times to question and try to reshape the environment, and there are times to adapt to the environment. Some creative people question so many things so often that others stop taking them seriously. Everyone has to learn which assumptions are worth questioning and how to pick the battles worth fighting. This is an important part of the analysis of a creative idea. Sometimes, it is better for individuals to leave the inconsequential assumptions alone so that they have an audience when they find something worth the fight.

Teachers should make questioning a part of the daily classroom exchange. It is more important for students to learn what questions to ask—and how to ask them—than it is for them to learn the answers. Teachers can help students evaluate their questions by discouraging the idea that the teacher asks questions and the students simply answer them. Teachers should avoid perpetuating the belief that the teacher's role is to teach students the facts. By helping students learn how to formulate good questions and how to answer questions, teachers can help students understand that what matters is their ability to use facts.

It's easy for teachers to make the pedagogical mistake of emphasizing the answering and not the asking of questions. The good student is perceived as the one who rapidly furnishes the right answers. The expert in a field thus becomes the extension of the expert student—the one who knows and can recite a lot of information. As Dewey (1933) recognized, how a person thinks is often more important than what a person thinks. Teachers need to teach students how to ask the right questions (good, thought-provoking, and interesting ones) and lessen the emphasis on rote learning.

Language arts (I–HS): Teachers can ask students to explain why the subject of a declarative sentence should precede the verb of that sentence.

Mathematics (I–HS): Teachers can encourage students to consider why the U.S. numeration system uses ten as a base.

Science (P–I): Teachers can request that students find out if a human's weight would be the same on other planets.

Social studies (P–HS): Teachers can ask students why people in U.S. society often say "Hello" when they answer the phone or first meet someone.

Foreign language (I–C): Teachers can encourage students to ponder what makes a given language foreign to someone.

Art (HS): Teachers can ask students to consider whether they could do a three-dimensional painting.

Music (P–C): Teachers can ask students to determine if a conversation could be viewed as music.

Physical education (P–HS): Teachers can encourage students to consider why people tend to root for hometown athletic teams.

Taking It to Heart

Teachers should give five examples of how they can help students question and analyze assumptions.

LESSON 10: SELL CREATIVE IDEAS

Targeted skill: Selling creative ideas

Prompt words or phrases: persuade, convince, argue for, advocate

People would like to assume that their wonderful, creative ideas are instantly obvious as brilliant and worthy. But, as Galileo, Edvard Munch, Toni Morrison, Sylvia Plath, and millions of others have discovered, ideas do not sell themselves; quite the contrary. Creative ideas are usually viewed with suspicion and distrust, and, many times, so are those who propose such ideas. Because people are comfortable with and probably have a vested interest in their existing ways of thinking, it can be extremely difficult to dislodge people from their current ways of thinking.

Using It in Life

Sticky notes are an ingenious invention that enables people to attach a note to a sheet of paper and then remove it. They have been an enormous commercial success. What many people don't realize is how difficult it was for the inventor of this product to persuade his superiors that the weak adhesive that attaches the note to a piece of paper would have a practical use. Similarly, when Sir Alexander Fleming first discovered the mold that would later prove to yield penicillin, his superiors were unconvinced that his discovery would have any commercial value.

Taking It to the Classroom

Students need to learn how to persuade other people of the value of their ideas. This selling is part of the practical aspect of creative thinking. If students do a science project, teachers should have them present it and show why it makes an important contribution. If students create a piece of artwork, teachers should ask them to explain why they think it has value. If students have a plan for a new form of government, teachers should ask them explain why it is better than the existing form of government. At times it may be necessary for teachers to justify their ideas about teaching to a principal. Teachers should prepare their students for the same kinds of experiences.

Language arts (P–I): Teachers can ask students to convince a classmate to read a book.

Mathematics (P–HS): Teachers can encourage students to convince their classmates that their methods of solving math problems are correct.

Science (I–C): Teachers can prompt students to formulate an interpretation of scientific data and convince others that their interpretation is correct.

Social studies (I–HS): Teachers can ask students to imagine that they are presidential candidates and persuade people to vote for them.

Foreign language (HS): Teachers can encourage students to develop arguments regarding why it is worthwhile to study a foreign language.

Art (I–C): Teachers can request that students convince someone of the value of a piece of artwork they have created.

Music (HS): Teachers can tell students to give reasons why rap music is good or not good for the development of teenagers.

Physical education (P–I): Teachers can encourage students to devise a game and then convince others that it will be fun to play.

Taking It to Heart

Teachers should give five examples of how to help students practice selling their creative ideas in a classroom.

LESSON 11: GENERATE IDEAS

Targeted skill: Generating ideas

Prompt words or phrases: generate, create, originate, spawn, produce, think up

Sometimes an idea strikes when it is least expected. Sometimes one needs to invest a long time in developing an idea. Researchers have investigated how ideas come around and what constitutes novel ideas. It turns out that the first step in generating ideas is to be unafraid to generate them! Thus, it is very important to teach students how to be open and excited about the task of originating new ideas.

Using It in Life

Generating ideas has become a routine part of everyday life precisely because everyday life has become so nonroutine. For example, on a recent trip, a traveler was in a hotel room and needed to travel to Fribourg, Switzerland. Such a trip would be routine if there were a commercial airport in Fribourg, but there isn't. So the traveler had to figure out where to fly to get to Fribourg. How does a person figure out this dilemma without the benefit of an atlas? This individual started generating ideas, as all people do when faced with a nonroutine problem. He called a travel agent, who was not able to help him. He tried calling an airline, but the clerk couldn't provide him with an answer. Ditto for another airline. Finally he tried one Internet site after another until he found a site for the University of Fribourg, which included a map indicating that the nearest airport was in Geneva. The point is that he needed to generate many ideas, most of which failed, until he finally solved his problem.

Taking It to the Classroom

Creative people show a "legislative" style of thinking: they like to generate ideas to do things their own way and to make their own plans rather than have someone else do these things for them (Sternberg, 1997b). An environment for generating ideas can be constructively critical, but it must not be harshly or destructively critical. Students need to acknowledge that some ideas are better than others. Teachers and students can collaborate to identify and encourage any creative aspects of ideas that are presented. When suggested ideas don't seem to have much value, it's important that teachers do more than just criticize. Rather, teachers should suggest new approaches, preferably ones that incorporate at least some aspects of the previous ideas that in themselves didn't seem to have much value. (This is a good place for using the skill of redefining the problem.) Teachers should praise students for generating many ideas, regardless of whether some seem silly or unrelated, while encouraging them to identify and develop their best ideas into high-quality projects.

Language arts (P–C): Teachers can ask students to write a poem.

Mathematics (P–C): Teachers can request that students create a mathematical word problem.

Science (P–C): Teachers can encourage students to propose a simple experiment.

Social studies (I): Teachers can have students suggest a student government structure for a classroom.

Foreign language (P-I): Teachers can ask students to invent a way to put their communications into a code (analogous to pig latin).

Art (P–HS): Teachers can encourage students to decide on a still life arrangement to draw.

Music (P–I): Teachers can ask students to invent a tune.

Physical education (P–I): Teachers can ask students to invent a game.

Taking It to Heart

Teachers should give five examples of how students can use idea generation in a classroom.

LESSON 12: RECOGNIZE THE TWO FACES OF KNOWLEDGE

Targeted skill: Understanding that knowledge is two edged

Prompt words or phrases: prevent entrenchment, maintain flexibility, avoid getting boxed in, stay open-minded

On the one hand, individuals cannot be creative without knowledge. Quite simply, individuals can't go beyond their existing state of knowledge if they don't know what that state is. Many students have ideas that are creative for them but not creative for their field, because others have had the same ideas before. Teachers have the advantage that their greater knowledge base enables them to be creative in ways that students, who are still learning about the basics of the field, cannot be.

On the other hand, knowledge can create its own limitations. The knowledge held by experts can lead these experts to tunnel vision, narrow thinking, and entrenchment. Experts can become so stuck in one way of thinking that they are unable to extricate themselves from it. Such narrow thinking can happen to anyone. For example, people who are used to speaking in a native language sometimes find that their native language actually interferes when they try to learn a second language. They are so used to the way things are done in the first language that learning a new way of doing things is hard. That is why, for Americans, Chinese is harder to learn than Spanish. Much of what we learned when we learned English helps us in Spanish, but it may actually interfere with our learning Chinese, because the rules in the Chinese language are so different.

Using It in Life

Some years ago, I had an experience that demonstrates how knowledge can be a two-edged sword. I was visiting a very famous psychologist who lives outside the United States, and as part of the tour the psychologist had planned, I was invited to visit the local zoo. At the zoo, we passed the primate cages. As it happened, just then the primates were engaged in what euphemistically could be called strange and unnatural sexual behavior. I averted my eyes; however, my host did not. After he observed the primates for a short time, I was astounded to hear him give an analysis of the sexual behavior of the primates in terms of his own theory of intelligence. I realized at that time, as I has many times since, how knowledge and expertise can be a double-edged sword. Although the psychologist knew about human intelligence, his theory was not relevant at all to primate behavior.

Taking It to the Classroom

Learning must be a lifelong process, not a process that terminates when an individual achieves some measure of recognition. When people believe they know everything there is to know, they are unlikely to ever show truly meaningful creativity again. Individuals need to realize that the teaching-learning process is a two-way street. Teachers have as much to learn from their students as their students have to learn from them. Teachers have knowledge students do not have, but students have flexibility—precisely because they do not know as much as teachers. Teachers should not believe they know it all. Teachers can open up channels for creativity by learning from as well as teaching to their students.

Language arts (HS): Teachers can ask students to envision a different side to a literary character they have viewed in a certain way (e.g., a dark side to a character who seems helpful and friendly).

Mathematics (P–C): Teachers can encourage students to consider a type of math problem they have always solved one way and solve it another way.

Science (HS–C): Teachers can prompt students to consider an alternative explanation for a generally accepted scientific phenomenon.

Social studies (HS–C): Teachers can ask students to consider a new service a town government might offer that it is not currently offering.

Foreign language (HS–C): Teachers can request that students find a new way of saying something in a foreign language that they now say in a particular way.

Art (I–HS): Teachers can ask students to contemplate how comics defy the conventions of most great art.

Music (HS–C): Teachers can help students decide how Chinese opera defies the conventions of Western opera.

Physical education (P–HS): Teachers can ask students to consider what makes a game a game.

Taking It to Heart

Teachers should give five examples of how to help students use their understanding that knowledge is two edged.

LESSON 13: IDENTIFY AND SURMOUNT OBSTACLES

Targeted skill: Identifying and overcoming obstacles

Prompt words or phrases: surmount, overcome, persevere, keep trying, persist, don't give up

Buying low and selling high means defying the crowd. And people who defy the crowd—those who think creatively—almost inevitably encounter resistance. The question is not whether one will encounter obstacles—obstacles will surely be encountered. The question is whether the creative thinker has the fortitude to persevere. It seems that so many people start their careers doing creative work and then vanish from the radar screen. Perhaps at least one reason why so many promising young creative thinkers disappear is that sooner or later they decide that being creative is not worth the resistance and punishment. Truly creative thinkers are willing to pay a short-term price because they recognize they can make a difference in the long run. But often it takes a long time before the value of a creative idea is recognized and appreciated.

Using It in Life

When I was very young, I became interested in intelligence and intelligence testing because I had achieved poor scores on intelligence tests. As a seventh-grader, I decided it would be interesting to do a science project on intelligence testing. I found the Stanford-Binet Intelligence Scales in the adult section of the town library and started giving the test to friends. Unfortunately, one of my friends tattled to his mother, and she reported me to the school authorities. The head school psychologist threatened to burn the book that contained the test if I ever brought the book into school again and suggested that I find another interest. Had I done so, I never would have done all the work on intelligence that has meant a great deal to my life and, I hope, something to the world. The school psychologist's opinion presented a major obstacle, especially to me as an early adolescent, but it was a surmountable obstacle that did not deter me from my interests and my future profession.

Taking It to the Classroom

To show students that obstacles don't confront only them, teachers should describe obstacles that they, their friends, and well-known figures have faced while trying to be creative. Teachers should include stories about people who were not supportive, about bad grades for unwelcome ideas, and about frosty receptions to what may have been the best ideas. To help students deal with obstacles, teachers can remind them of the many creative people whose ideas were initially shunned and help them develop an inner sense of awe for the creative act. They can also suggest that students reduce their concern over what others think. However, teachers should remember that it is often difficult for students to lessen their dependence on the opinions of their peers.

When a student attempts to surmount an obstacle, the effort should be praised, even if the student is not entirely successful. Teachers should point out aspects of the student's approach that were successful and discuss why they were, and then suggest other ways to confront similar obstacles. Teachers can also ask the class to brainstorm ways to confront a given obstacle to get students thinking about the many strategies people can use to confront problems. Some obstacles are within oneself, such as performance anxiety. Other obstacles are external, such as others' bad opinions of what one does. Whether internal or external, obstacles must be surmounted.

Language arts (I–C): Teachers can encourage students to present a unique style of poetry in a way that may appeal to critics.

Mathematics (I): Teachers can ask students to compare a novel way to solve a multiplication problem to the common method, and improve the novel method so that it is more efficient than the common method.

Science (P–HS): Teachers can work with students to review the approved lab procedure for a new experiment to make sure it is safe.

Social studies (I–C): Teachers can ask students to suggest alternative explanations for historical events that most others interpret differently.

Foreign language (I–C): Teachers can encourage students to persist in learning a language when they feel like giving up.

Art (P): Teachers can encourage students to persist in working on a difficult art assignment.

Music (P–I): Teachers can help students learn a difficult song that requires a lot of practice.

Physical education (P–HS): Teachers can ask students to work out in preparation for an athletic competition.

Taking It to Heart

Teachers should list five examples of how to help students practice identifying and surmounting obstacles in a classroom.

LESSON 14: TAKE SENSIBLE RISKS

Targeted skill: Taking risks sensibly

Prompt words or phrases: take sensible risks, try new approaches, venture into the unknown, take a chance

When creative people defy the crowd by buying low and selling high, they take risks in much the same way as people who invest do. Some of these investments simply don't pan out. Moreover, defying the crowd means risking the crowd's wrath. However, there are more and less sensible reasons to defy the crowd. Creative people take sensible risks and produce ideas that others ultimately admire and respect as trendsetting. In taking these risks, creative people sometimes make mistakes, fail, and fall flat on their faces.

Using It in Life

Nearly every major discovery or invention entailed some risk. When a movie theater was the only place to see a movie, someone created the idea of the home video industry. Skeptics wondered if anyone would want to see movies on a small screen. Another initially risky idea was the home computer. People wondered if anyone would have enough use for a home computer to justify the cost. These ideas were once risks but have now been ingrained into U.S. society.

I took a risk as an assistant professor when I decided to study intelligence, because the field of intelligence has low prestige within the academic field of psychology. When I was being considered for tenure, it came to my attention that my university was receiving letters that questioned why it would want to give tenure to someone in such a marginal and unprestigious field. I suspected that I had made a mistake when I stated that my work was about intelligence. Indeed, I could have done essentially the same work but labeled my field "thinking" or "problem-solving"—fields with much more prestige. I then sought the advice of a mentor, who told me that he had come to Yale wanting to make a difference to the field of perception, and he *had* made a difference. The mentor went on to say that now I was afraid my decision might cost me my job. I realized that I had taken a risk. But there was only one thing I felt I could do—exactly what I was doing. If this field meant so much to me, then I needed to pursue it, just as I was doing, even if it meant losing my job. Fortunately, I didn't lose my job. However, other risks I have taken have not paid off. When taking risks, individuals must realize that some of the situations just won't work out—that is sometimes the cost of doing creative work.

Taking It to the Classroom

Although it is important to emphasize sensible risk taking, this type of risk taking is not about risking life and limb. To help students learn to take sensible risks and to develop a sense of how to assess risks, teachers should encourage them to take some intellectual risks with courses, activities, and teachers.

Few students are willing to take risks in school because they learn that such risks can be costly. Perfect test scores and conventional papers often receive praise and open up possibilities for the future. Failure to attain a certain academic standard is perceived as originating from a lack of ability and motivation and may lead to scorn and to the loss of possibilities. Students don't want to risk taking hard courses or saying things teachers may not like when these behaviors might lead to low grades or even failure. Teachers may inadvertently encourage students to learn to play it safe when they give assignments without choices and allow only particular answers to questions. Thus, teachers need to not only encourage sensible risk taking, but also reward it.

> **Language arts (P–I):** Teachers can encourage students to choose to read the more difficult of two books.

> **Mathematics (HS):** Teachers can encourage students to try to solve a geometric proof that appears difficult.

> **Science (HS–C):** Teachers can describe a published experiment and challenge students to figure out what is wrong with it.

> **Social studies (P–HS):** Teachers can suggest that students describe things in their own country that don't work the way they're supposed to.

> **Foreign language (HS):** Teachers can encourage students to learn the basics of a difficult foreign language before traveling to a country where that language is spoken so they can speak to the residents in their own language.

> **Art (P–HS):** Teachers can help students learn to use a new artistic medium that is difficult to master.

> **Music (I–C):** Teachers can encourage students to perform in a recital attended by a large audience.

> **Physical education (P–HS):** Teachers can ask students to play a position in baseball that they have not played before.

Taking It to Heart

Teachers should give five examples of how they can help students practice taking sensible risks in a classroom.

LESSON 15: TOLERATE AMBIGUITY

Targeted skill: Tolerating ambiguity

Prompt words or phrases: tolerate, allow, consent to, endure, put up with

A creative idea tends to come in bits and pieces and develops over time. But the period in which the idea is developing tends to be uncomfortable. Without time or the ability to tolerate ambiguity, individuals may jump to a less than optimal solution.

Using It in Life

People like things to be black and white. They like to think that a country is good or bad (ally or enemy), or that a given idea in education works or does not work. The problem is that there are a lot of grays in creative work. Artists working on new paintings and writers working on new books often report feeling scattered and unsure in their thoughts; they need to figure out whether they are even on the right track. Scientists are often not sure whether theories they have developed are exactly correct. They need to tolerate ambiguity and uncertainty until they get their ideas just right. People who are trying to improve their relationships with significant others often find that immediately after a change is made in a relationship, a period of uncomfortable ambiguity follows. They may be tempted to regress to the way things were before, but they are often better off when they tolerate the ambiguity long enough to let the change take root.

Taking It to the Classroom

Tolerating ambiguity is difficult. When a student has almost the right topic for a paper or almost the right science project, it is tempting for teachers to accept the near miss. To help students become creative, teachers can encourage them to accept and extend the period in which their ideas do not quite converge. Teachers can teach them that uncertainty and its attendant discomfort is part of living a creative life. Ultimately, they will benefit from tolerating ambiguity by coming up with better ideas.

Language arts (I–C): Teachers can encourage students to refine an idea for a short story that is not yet quite formed.

Mathematics (P–C): Teachers can ask students to keep trying to solve a problem they have not yet solved in its entirety.

Science (P): Teachers can encourage students to figure out what makes plants grow.

Social studies (HS–C): Teachers can help students examine why the United States entered the Iraq War.

Foreign language (I–C): Teachers can encourage students to figure out the meaning of a word from the context of the sentence.

Art (P–I): Teachers can ask students to figure out the value of an abstract piece of modern art.

Music (I–C): Teachers can encourage students to examine why people enjoy dissonant music.

Physical education (P–I): Teachers can ask students to play a game with which they are familiar, such as football, using new rules.

Taking It to Heart

Teachers should give five examples of how they can encourage students to use the skill of tolerating ambiguity in a classroom.

LESSON 16: BUILD SELF-EFFICACY

Targeted skill: Building self-efficacy

Prompt words or phrases: believe in your ability to (a) get the job done, (b) do what you need to do, (c) work effectively, (d) achieve your goals

People sometimes reach a point where they feel that no one believes in, values, or even appreciates them or what they are doing. Because creative work often does not get a warm reception, it is extremely important that creative people believe in the value of what they are doing. This is not to say that individuals should believe that every idea they have is a good idea. Rather, it is to say that individuals need to believe that, ultimately, they have the ability to make a difference.

Using It in Life

When the time comes to start a project of one kind or another, sometimes people find themselves paralyzed. The project seems so large and overwhelming that they're not even sure where or how to begin. Thus, people sometimes feel incapable of ever getting the project going. A good solution to such paralysis is for individuals to start the project with the smallest or easiest step possible. Then they take on the next smallest or easiest step, and so on. In this way, they build a sense of their self-efficacy by showing themselves that they are indeed capable of getting the job done. Eventually the project is well under way.

Taking It to the Classroom

The main limitation on what students can do is what they think they can do. All students have the capacity to be creators and to experience the joy associated with making something new, but first they must have a strong belief in their creativity. Sometimes teachers and parents unintentionally limit what students can do by sending messages that express or imply limits on students' potential accomplishments. Instead, teachers and parents should help students believe in their ability to be creative.

Probably the best predictor of success among students is not their ability, but their belief in their ability to succeed. If students are encouraged to succeed and to believe in their own ability to succeed, they will very likely find the success that would otherwise elude them.

Language arts (I–C): Teachers can tell students to read a book that is very difficult, but not beyond their understanding.

Mathematics (HS): Teachers can encourage students to spend a lot of time solving a difficult extra-credit trigonometry problem.

Science (HS–C): Teachers can encourage students to keep trying to complete a physics experiment until they get it right.

Social studies (HS–C): Teachers can convince students that they can eventually understand the U.S. judicial system well enough to explain it to their classmates.

Foreign language (I–C): Teachers can encourage students to set high goals for the number of vocabulary words to learn during a week.

Art (I–HS): Teachers can suggest to students that they choose a challenging subject to sculpt.

Music (P–C): Teachers can convince students that it is possible to play very difficult pieces if they practice enough.

Physical education (HS–C): Teachers can encourage students to set the goal of running a half marathon at the end of a semester of track class.

Taking It to Heart

Teachers should give five examples of how to build self-efficacy in a classroom.

LESSON 17: UNCOVER TRUE INTERESTS

Targeted skill: Recognizing a true interest

Prompt words or phrases: find yourself, discover who you are, uncover your passion, know what to do and where to go

To unleash students' best creative performances, teachers can help them find what excites them. This may not be the same for everyone. People who truly excel creatively in any pursuit, whether vocational or avocational, almost always genuinely love what they do. Certainly, the most creative people are intrinsically motivated in their work (Amabile, 1996). Less creative people often pick a career for the money or prestige and are bored with or loathe their career. These people do not do work that makes a difference in their field.

Using It in Life

An incident from my life is a perfect example of enthusiasm for a project, although by the wrong person. When my son, Seth, was young, I was heartened that Seth wanted to play the piano, especially since I like the piano and play the piano myself. But then Seth stopped practicing and ultimately quit. A short time thereafter, he informed me that he had decided he wanted to play the trumpet. My initial reaction was very negative as I pointed out to Seth that he had already quit the piano and probably would quit the trumpet too.

I then found myself wondering why I had been so harsh and had said such a thing. But then, I understood it. If someone else's child wanted to play the trumpet, fine. But I couldn't imagine a Sternberg child playing the trumpet. It didn't fit my image of a Sternberg kid. I realized I was being narrow-minded and doing exactly the opposite of what I had told everyone else to do. It is one thing to talk the talk, another to walk the walk. I backpedaled, and Seth started playing the trumpet.

Later on, Seth did, in fact, quit the trumpet. But he did eventually find the right thing. A number of years later, he became a college student and started two businesses. Businesses? *My* son? Seth is doing what is right for him. Whether it is right for me just does not matter. Today, in 2007, Seth is an entepreneur—his choice, not mine.

Taking It to the Classroom

Helping students find what they really love to do is often hard and frustrating work. Yet sharing the frustration with students now is better than leaving them to face it alone later. To help students uncover their true interests, teachers can ask them to demonstrate a special talent or ability for the class. Teachers should explain that it does not matter what they do (within reason), only that they love the activity.

When working with students, it is important that teachers help them find what interests them, even if it doesn't particularly interest everyone else. Often, enthusiasm is infectious and others are drawn into new areas of pursuit.

Students often pursue a certain field not because it is what they want to do, but because it is what their parents or other authority figures expect them to do, just as I expected Seth to play the piano. This is a sad state for these students, because although they may do good work in that field, they almost certainly will not do great work. It is hard for people to do great work in a field that does not interest them.

Language arts (P–I): Teachers can encourage students to identify their favorite author.

Mathematics (I–HS): Teachers can encourage students to figure out uses of math in sports.

Science (P–C): Teachers can support students in designing a science project around some problem that really interests them.

Social studies (P): Teachers can have students design a poster showing the accomplishments of a president whom they particularly admire.

Foreign language (I–C): Teachers can encourage students to study the language of a country whose culture really appeals to them.

Art (I): Teachers can encourage students to do a painting in the style of an artist whose work they really enjoy.

Music (P–HS): Teachers can have students bring a recording of their favorite kind of music to class and discuss why the music appeals to them.

Physical education (P): Teachers can ask students to design games that would be fun to play.

Taking It to Heart

Teachers should give five examples of how to help students find what they love to do.

LESSON 18: DELAY GRATIFICATION

Targeted skill: Delaying gratification

Prompt words or phrases: wait, delay, defer, postpone, put off, procrastinate

Part of being creative is being able to work on a project or task for a long time without immediate or interim rewards. Creative people must learn that rewards are not always immediate and that there are benefits to delaying gratification. When people do creative work, they are often ignored or even punished in the short term for doing so. An important part of the discipline of creative work is to learn to wait for rewards. The greatest rewards are often those that are delayed.

Using It in Life

One of my greatest rewards has yet to come! Some years ago, I contracted with a publisher to develop a test of intelligence based on the theory of intelligence (Sternberg, 1985) used in this book. Things were going well until a new president took over the company. In short order, the project was canceled. The company's perception was that there wasn't a profitable market for a test of intelligence based on the theory of analytical, creative, and practical abilities. I disagreed.

Whoever may have been right, my coauthor, Elena Grigorenko, and I ultimately decided that if we wanted to make this test available, we would have to do it ourselves, not through a conventional publisher. So now, some years later, we are still working to realize the test in a way that others can use it. It is a difficult exercise in delay of gratification, but we try to practice what we preach—and so we wait for the day when the test will make a difference in students' lives.

Taking It to the Classroom

Teachers can give students examples of delayed gratification from their lives and the lives of creative individuals and help them apply these examples to their lives.

Many people believe that students should be rewarded immediately and expect rewards for good performance. This style of teaching and parenting emphasizes the here and now and often comes at the expense of what is best in the long term. Hard work often does not bring immediate rewards. Students do not immediately become expert basketball players, dancers, musicians, or sculptors. The reward of becoming an expert seems far away, and many times students succumb to the temptations of the moment—watching television or playing video games. The people who make the most of their abilities are those who wait for a reward and recognize that few serious challenges are met in a moment. Ninth-grade students may not see the benefits of hard work, but the advantages of a solid academic performance will be obvious when those students apply to college.

The short-term focus of most school assignments does little to teach students the value of delaying gratification. Projects are clearly superior in meeting this goal, but it is difficult for teachers to assign home projects if they are not confident of parental involvement and support. By working on a task for many weeks or months, a student learns the value of making incremental efforts for long-term gains.

Language arts (I–C): Teachers can encourage students to finish a massive writing assignment by completing it in increments.

Mathematics (HS): Teachers can prompt students to solve a complicated algebra equation by breaking it down into a series of smaller, simpler equations and plugging the resulting numbers into the complicated equation.

Science (P–I): Teachers can ask students to keep a log of how an avocado grows.

Social studies (HS): Teachers can tell students that, before they explain the outcome of a particular World War II battle, they should research the circumstances of the various troops involved.

Foreign language (I–C): Teachers can ask students to contemplate the long-term benefits of learning a foreign language.

Art (P–I): Teachers can encourage students to undertake one long-term art project to complete by the end of the school term.

Music (I–C): Teachers can ask students to practice a piece until they are able to play it almost perfectly.

Physical education (P–C): Teachers can encourage students to practice very hard for an upcoming game.

Taking It to Heart

Teachers should give five examples of how to help students practice delaying gratification.

LESSON 19: MODEL CREATIVITY

Targeted skill: Modeling creativity

Prompt words or phrases: model, exemplify, demonstrate, develop, promote, encourage

There are many ways an environment can foster creativity (Sternberg & Williams, 1996). Although this lesson is targeted to teachers modeling creativity, students may also promote and demonstrate creativity to their classmates.

Using It in Life

The teachers most remembered from school days are not those who crammed the most content into their lectures. The teachers remembered are those who, by their thoughts and actions, served as role models for their students. Most likely they balanced teaching content with teaching students how to think with and about that content. For example, I will never forget the teacher who started off seventh-grade social studies class by asking whether we knew what social studies was. Of course, we all nodded our heads to indicate that we did. But it took three class sessions to figure out just what it really was.

Another teacher asked the students in her class to decide on and then implement a form of government for the class. Students had an interesting and informative discussion of different forms of government, including their advantages and disadvantages. They then implemented their chosen form (a modified form of democracy). Instead of just telling the students advantages and disadvantages of various forms of government, the teacher let the students find out these things for themselves.

Occasionally, during a workshop on developing creativity, someone asks exactly what he should do to develop creativity. Bad start. To model creativity, teachers should think and teach creatively. Teachers should think carefully about their values, goals, and ideas about creativity and show them in their actions.

Taking It to the Classroom

Following are a number of techniques teachers can use to provide an environment that supports creative thinking.

Supporting Creative Thinking in the Classroom

- Model creativity
- Help students cross-fertilize their thinking
- Give students time to think creatively
- Instruct and assess for creativity
- Reward creativity
- Reward creative efforts
- Encourage creative collaboration
- Help students imagine other viewpoints

Model creativity. The most powerful way for teachers to develop creativity in students is to model creativity. Children develop creativity not when they are told to, but when they are shown how. Teachers who demonstrate creative thinking in their actions give students permission to be creative. Leading by example is one of the strongest environmental influences available to a teacher.

Help students to cross-fertilize their thinking—to think across subjects and disciplines. The traditional school environment often has separate classrooms and classmates for different subjects. This seems to encourage the view that learning occurs in discrete boxes—the math box, the social studies box, the science box. However, creative ideas and insights often result from integrating material across subject areas, not from memorizing and reciting material. Teaching students to cross-fertilize draws on their skills, interests, and abilities, regardless of the subject. For example, if students have trouble understanding math, teachers should ask them to draft test questions related to their special interests. This means asking the baseball fan to devise geometry problems based on the game. The context may spur creative ideas because the student finds the topic (baseball) enjoyable, which may counteract some of the anxiety caused by geometry. Cross-fertilization motivates students who are not interested in subjects taught in the abstract.

One way teachers can enact cross-fertilization in the classroom is to ask students to identify their best and worst academic areas. Teachers can then ask students to come up with project ideas in their weak areas based on ideas borrowed from one of their strongest areas. For example, students can apply their interest in science to social studies by analyzing the scientific aspects of trends in national politics.

Give students time to think creatively. The United States is a society in a hurry. As a group, U.S. residents eat fast food, rush from one place to another, and value quickness. Indeed, one way to say someone is smart is to say that the person is *quick* (Sternberg, 1985), a clear indication of an emphasis on time.

Just look at the format of standardized tests—many multiple-choice problems squeezed into a brief time slot. Most creative insights, however, do not happen in a rush (Gruber & Davis, 1988). Time is needed to understand a problem and to toss it around. If people are asked to think creatively, they need time to do it well. If questions are stuffed into tests or students are given more homework than they can complete, they won't have time to think creatively.

Instruct and assess for creativity. If given multiple-choice tests only, students quickly learn the type of thinking that is valued, no matter what is said. To encourage creativity, teachers can include at least some opportunities for creative thought in assignments and tests. They can do this by asking questions that require factual recall, analytical thinking, and creative thinking. For example, students might be asked to learn about a law, analyze the law, and then think about how the law might be improved.

Reward creativity. It is not enough for teachers to talk about the value of creativity. Students are accustomed to authority figures saying one thing and doing another. They are exquisitely sensitive to what teachers value when it comes to the bottom line, namely, the grade or evaluation. Teachers need to "put their money where their mouths are," or students will go with the money—that is, the grade.

Reward creative efforts. In addition to rewarding creativity, teachers should reward efforts toward creativity. For example, teachers can assign a project and remind students to demonstrate their knowledge, analytical and writing skills, and creativity. Students should understand that creativity does not depend on a teacher's agreement with what they write, but rather on their expressing ideas in a way that represents a synthesis between existing ideas and their own thoughts. Teachers should care only that the ideas are creative from the student's perspective, not necessarily creative with regard to the state of the art. Students may generate an idea that someone else has expressed already.

Some teachers complain that they cannot grade creative responses with as much objectivity as they can apply to multiple-choice or short-answer responses, and it is true that there is some sacrifice of objectivity with these types of questions. However, research shows that evaluators are remarkably consistent in their assessment of creativity (Amabile, 1996; Sternberg & Lubart, 1995a). If the goal of assessment is to instruct students, then it is better for teachers to ask for creative work and evaluate it with somewhat less objectivity than to evaluate students exclusively on uncreative work. Teachers should let students know that there is no completely objective way to evaluate creativity.

Encourage creative collaboration. Creative performance is often viewed as a solitary occupation—an author sitting alone writing in a studio, an artist painting in a solitary loft, or a musician practicing endlessly in a small music room. In reality, people often work in groups, as collaboration can spur creativity.

Teachers can encourage students to learn by example by collaborating with creative people.

Help students imagine things from other viewpoints. An essential aspect of working with other people and getting the most out of collaborative creative activity is imagining oneself in other people's shoes. Perspectives are broadened when individuals learn to see the world from different points of view. Teachers can encourage students to see the importance of understanding, respecting, and responding to other people's points of view. This is important, as many bright and potentially creative students never achieve success because they don't develop practical intelligence (Sternberg, 1985, 1997a). They may do well in school and on tests, but they never seem to learn how to get along with others or to see things and themselves as others see them.

Language arts (I–HS): Teachers can tell students to write short stories based on their favorite hobbies.

Mathematics (HS): Teachers can have students write math problems based on a sport that interests them.

Science (P–I): Teachers can ask students to discuss how science can be seen as an art, especially when new materials such as Styrofoam are created.

Social studies (I–HS): Teachers can encourage students to discuss how clothing styles reflect the cultural values of a given time.

Foreign language (I–C): Teachers can have students develop a skit in a foreign language they are learning.

Art (P): Teachers can ask students to choose their own subject and make a clay model of it.

Music (P–I): Teachers can have students write new words for an existing song.

Physical education (P–I): Teachers can ask students to invent a new exercise to stretch a particular group of muscles.

Taking It to Heart

Teachers should give five examples of how they can model creativity in a classroom.

**LESSON 20: ADDITIONAL PROMPTS FOR
                       CREATIVE THINKING**

Targeted skill: Creativity

Prompt words or phrases: create, imagine, suppose . . . then . . . , invent, discover, formulate

In this chapter, twelve simple lessons, devised by Sternberg, together with Lubart and Williams (Sternberg & Lubart, 1995a, 1995b; Sternberg & Williams, 1996), have been presented. Any teacher can foster creativity in students or in herself. However, it is important that teachers remember that the development of creativity is a lifelong process, not one that ends with a particular high school or university degree. After a person has a major creative idea, it is easy for him to spend the rest of his career following up on it. It is frightening to contemplate that the next idea may not be as good as the previous one, or that success may disappear with the next idea. The result is that an individual can become complacent and stop being creative. Teachers and administrators are susceptible to this, as well as to becoming victims of their own expertise—to becoming entrenched in ways of thinking that worked in the past but will not necessarily work in the future (Frensch & Sternberg, 1989). Being creative means stepping outside the boxes, whether created by oneself or by others, and continuing to do so throughout life.

Some additional prompts that teachers can use with students in teaching for creative thinking are given here. These prompts present activities with a larger context that require the use of a number of creative thinking skills.

Language Arts

- Teachers can encourage students to create a poem.
- Teachers can ask students what they might write if they wrote a contemporary ending to *Wuthering Heights*.
- Teachers can ask students to imagine what the effect on communication would be if a language existed without any grammar.
- Teachers can ask students to tell an original story.

Mathematics

- Teachers can ask students to invent a new number operation and explain how it works.
- Teachers can encourage students to contemplate what the effects on society would be if mathematics were to suddenly disappear from the contemporary scene.

- Teachers can have students comment on what the effect on society would be if people did all their mathematics using Roman numerals.
- Teachers can teach students modular "clock" arithmetic.

Science

- Teachers can ask students to formulate a theory that accounts for why the sky is blue.
- Teachers can ask students what they think the effects on the earth will be in 100 years if the ozone layer continues to be depleted at the current rate.
- Teachers can encourage students to comment on what life would be like if they lived on a planet that had double the gravitational force of the earth.
- Teachers can ask students what challenges they believe astronauts face in their lives.

Social Studies

- Teachers can ask students to formulate a constitution for a new country, modeling it after (but not copying) existing constitutions.
- Teachers can ask students to contemplate what kind of society they think the United States would have today if the colonies had not rebelled against Great Britain in 1776.
- Teachers can ask students to comment on what the world would be like today if Nazi Germany had won World War II.
- Teachers can ask students to set up a classroom government.

Foreign Language

- Teachers can encourage students to create a skit that shows what happens when a U.S. citizen first arrives at the Frankfurt airport.
- Teachers can ask students what differences they would expect to find in the world if everyone spoke the same language.
- Teachers can ask students to comment on how their lives would be different if they were living in a rural village in the south of France.

Art

- Teachers can encourage students to create sculptures on topics of their own choosing.
- Teachers can ask students to imagine that they have invented their own styles of painting and comment on what these styles look like.
- Teachers can ask students to comment on what kind of art they would display if they were to open their own art museum.
- Teachers can have children draw something of their own choosing with crayons.

Music

- Teachers can encourage students to invent new music forms and explain what they are.
- Teachers can ask students to imagine that Beethoven is alive and composing today and determine the effect his living in today's world has on the kind of music he composes.
- Teachers can ask students to comment on how they personally would be affected if musical accomplishments were the basis for establishing people's positions in society.

Physical Education

- Teachers can encourage students to create a new game that uses a soccer ball but has rules different from those of soccer.
- Teachers can ask students to think of how the game of baseball would be affected if the bases were moved two feet closer together.
- Teachers can ask students to comment on how society would be affected if the game of football were to disappear.
- Teachers can have children imagine what it would be like if the same team in professional basketball always won all its games.

Taking It to Heart

Teachers should give a few examples of how to use these creative prompts in teaching.

Teaching For Practical Thinking

Everyone fails sometimes. Indeed, it is doubtful that a person could ever learn if he or she never failed at anything. The sign of good, practical thinking is not that a person never makes mistakes, but rather that he or she learns from those mistakes so that the mistakes are not made again and again. A good thinker can be forgiven for making mistakes, but perhaps not for making the same mistakes repeatedly.

Almost everyone knows seemingly good thinkers who too often make mistakes and fail at what they do. It is as though their good thinking is for naught when they confront practical, real-world problems. Clearly, good thinking is not enough for successful performance in the everyday world, no matter how broadly good thinking is defined. People can come into the world with some of the best intellectual gifts heredity has to offer, can be brought up in a highly advanced environment, can read a book such as this, and can practice their intellectual skill, but they can still routinely make a mess of their lives. Unless they can circumvent or otherwise bypass the stumbling blocks that get in the way of practical intellectual performance, they may find that most, if not all, of their intellectual gifts are of little value. Conversely, highly accomplished people generally succeed not only because of their natural talents, but also because of other personal qualities.

Teachers should consider the nineteen stumbling blocks (see boxed text below) that can get in the way of even the best thinkers (Sternberg, 1986; Sternberg & Spear-Swerling, 1996). For the most part, these stumbling blocks are not strictly intellectual ones. But if people can control these sorts of practical problems, then they can truly concentrate on developing their intellects, knowing that this development will reflect itself in improved task performance. Reviewing the nineteen impediments to the practical realization of good thinking makes it increasingly obvious why conventional intelligence tests, and perhaps even more broadly defined ones, can account for only a small proportion of the variance in real-world performance.

Stumbling Blocks to Practical Thinking

- Lack of motivation
- Lack of impulse control
- Lack of perseverance or excessive perseveration
- Using the wrong abilities
- Inability to translate thought into action
- Lack of product orientation
- Inability to complete tasks and to follow through
- Failure to initiate projects
- Fear of failure
- Procrastination
- Misattribution of blame
- Excessive self-pity
- Excessive dependency
- Wallowing in personal difficulties
- Distractibility and lack of concentration
- Spreading oneself too thin or too thick
- Inability or unwillingness to see the forest for the trees
- Lack of balance among analytical, creative, and practical thinking
- Too little or too much self-confidence

LESSON 21: BECOME MOTIVATED

Targeted skill: Motivating oneself

Prompt words or phrases: succeed, accomplish, achieve, motivate, excite, arouse, spur

Stumbling block: Lack of motivation. It scarcely matters what talents people have if they are not motivated to use them. In many, if not most, environments, motivation counts at least as much as intellectual skills in the attainment of success. The reason motivation is so important is that individuals within a given environment— for example, a classroom—tend to represent a relatively narrow range of ability but a much broader range of motivation. Motivation thus becomes a key source of individual variation in success. For some people, motivation comes from external sources: approval of peers, attainment of recognition, acquisition of money, or whatever. For others, motivation is internal, derived from their own satisfaction in a job well done. Most people are both internally and externally motivated in different proportions. Whatever the source of motivation, it is critical to the expression of intelligence and to success.

On the whole, it is probably preferable for motivation to be internally— rather than externally—generated, because external sources of motivation tend to be transient. As a result, people who are primarily externally motivated are likely to lose their motivation when the external sources of reward diminish or disappear. Internally motivated individuals are able to maintain their motivation over the rising and falling of external rewards. For instance, students who are motivated primarily by stars, stickers, or other tangible rewards often lose their motivation when the rewards are unavailable. In contrast, students who have an intrinsic interest in a topic have a natural motivation for learning that is more easily sustained.

Using It in Life

Many people believe that the critical element for giftedness is IQ or some other aspect of intelligence. Certainly intelligence is one aspect of giftedness. But a finding that has emerged in the research literature again and again is that the common thread in gifted people is an incredible drive to succeed in a domain, what Ellen Winner (1998) calls "rage for mastery." These individuals are not motivated just by rewards. They are motivated intrinsically by a love of what they do (Amabile, 1996). Many employers find that the best predictor of job success is not some kind of ability test score, but rather the sheer desire to work hard and see a job well done. Great geniuses are often more distinguished by intense hard work, concentration, and drive than by anything else (Steptoe, 1998).

Taking It to the Classroom

Part of the reason why teaching for successful intelligence works is because it increases student interest in the material being taught and hence increases students' motivation to learn. Some teachers believe they are doing their jobs if they present material in a coherent and straightforward way. However, if students are not motivated, they will not pay attention and will not listen. In this situation, teachers may believe they are teaching, but little learning is occurring in their classrooms.

Language arts (P–I): Teachers can encourage students to try new ways to brainstorm for writing a poem, even if they are experiencing writer's block.

Mathematics (P–HS): Teachers can encourage students to complete unassigned problems from the textbook to gain a better understanding of the material.

Science (P–HS): Teachers can encourage students to complete a complicated experiment, even after several unsuccessful attempts.

Social studies (HS): Teachers can ask students to gain an in-depth understanding of a complex problem in modern international relations, such as an economic or political problem.

Foreign language (HS–C): Teachers can encourage students to choose to learn a very difficult language because it interests them instead of choosing to learn a more conventional language.

Art (I–HS): Teachers can ask students to find an artist whose work they truly admire and report on that artist's work.

Music (P–C): Teachers can motivate students to continue to enter performance competitions until they win.

Physical education (P–HS): Teachers can encourage students to understand that practice is necessary to achieve excellence and to act on this understanding.

Taking It to Heart

Teachers should list five activities they can assign and discuss with students that will help them overcome any lack of motivation.

LESSON 22: CONTROL IMPULSES

Targeted skill: Controlling impulses

Prompt words or phrases: reflect, control, curb, restrain, regulate

Stumbling block: Lack of impulse control. There are times in life when people need to act impulsively, but impulsive behavior tends to detract from, rather than enhance, intellectual work. Teachers sometimes encounter students who are capable of doing excellent academic work but whose capabilities are largely unrealized due to their tendency to work impulsively and without reflection. In one of his earliest books, Thurstone (1924) claimed that a key feature of intelligent persons is their ability to control impulsive responses. Many years later, a comparative psychologist, Stenhouse (1973), independently came to the same conclusion. Habitual impulsiveness gets in the way of optimal intellectual performance by not allowing people to bring their full intellectual resources to bear on a problem. Although endless reflection is also clearly undesirable, people should not let themselves get carried away by the first solution that occurs to them in attempting to solve a problem. Better solutions may arise after further thought.

Using It in Life

I knew a successful executive in a publishing house who learned firsthand the value of impulse control. The executive was one of several candidates for a major promotion. When the phone call came from the CEO, the executive was chagrined to learn that he did not get the promotion. The executive impulsively disparaged his boss's choice of candidate for the promotion. In short order, the executive discovered that not only had he lost the promotion, but his impulsive remark was about to cost him the job he already had.

Taking It to the Classroom

Teachers can encourage students to control their impulses by rewarding them when they do so. Teachers can ask students to reflect rather than jump to conclusions and can indicate their approval of students' willingness to control themselves. Teachers need to be careful that they do not set up a reward system that inadvertently rewards impulsivity. For example, when teachers emphasize speed rather than accuracy in assignments, or always call on the first person to raise his or her hand, they may be rewarding the very behavior they wish to suppress.

Language arts (P–C): Teachers can encourage students to think and plan before they begin writing.

Mathematics (P–C): Teachers can tell students to review their work before handing it in to make sure there are no nonsensical answers.

Science (C): Teachers can encourage students to think about alternative explanations for an experimental result rather than just accepting the first explanation that comes to mind.

Social studies (I–HS): Teachers can ask students to put together an outline before writing a paper on the consequences of the cold war to make sure they cover all the important points.

Foreign language (I–HS): Teachers can tell students to refrain from guessing that a foreign word that *sounds* like a particular word in their language necessarily *means* the same thing.

Art (P–I): Teachers can ask students to make a sketch before starting a large painting project.

Music (P–HS): Teachers can tell students to resist giving up on a difficult piece when practicing becomes frustrating.

Physical education (P–C): Teachers can encourage students to curb their desire to take unnecessary physical risks to beat an opponent in a sports competition.

Taking It to Heart

Teachers should list five activities they can assign and discuss with students that will help them control their impulses.

LESSON 23: PERSEVERE, BUT DON'T PERSEVERATE

Targeted skill: Knowing when to hold and when to fold

Prompt words or phrases: balance, weigh, assess, continue, pursue, persist, keep on, carry through versus quit, cease, desist, give up

Stumbling block: Lack of perseverance or excessive perseveration. Some people, despite all their intelligence, give up too easily. If things don't immediately go their way, or if their initial attempts at something are unsuccessful, they drop whatever they're doing. They thereby lose the opportunity to complete—possibly in a highly suitable way—the tasks they undertake. The smallest frustration is enough to keep them from persevering.

At the other end of the spectrum are people who continue working on a problem long after they should have quit. They perseverate even after it should be clear to them that they are not able to solve the problem, at least at the moment. Or perhaps they have already solved the problem but go on to solve it again and again.

Using It in Life

The existence of a tendency toward perseveration is evident in certain scholarly careers. The scholar creates an important piece of work, perhaps as her doctoral dissertation, then follows up the work with studies that address the more minor problems that evolve out of that initial work. At some point, people in the field expect that scholar to move on to another problem, or at least take a different approach to the same problem. Instead, the scholar continues to do what to most people appears to be the same research, over and over again. There may be minor changes in or additions to the research, but from the point of view of everyone but the scholar, her scholarly contribution ceased long ago.

Perseveration occurs in other areas of life as well. Almost everyone knows someone who, having been rejected repeatedly by a potential romantic partner, nevertheless keeps trying again and again, despite the persistence of negative signals from the potential partner. It is as though the person is unable to end his fruitless quest. He perseverates long after it has become obvious to everyone else, and sometimes even to himself, that he is making no headway.

Of course, some people give up when they shouldn't. Writers, for example, often give up after they receive a few rejections of their manuscript. Some years ago, a professor gave up on a manuscript that had been rejected by a few journals. He concluded the manuscript was just not publishable. Ten years later, he was cleaning out his files and discovered the manuscript, which had been rejected multiple times. He reread the manuscript and found that he still believed the manuscript had value. He resubmitted the manuscript to another journal, and it was accepted with a request for just one revision—updating of the references, which were all at least ten years old!

Taking It to the Classroom

Teachers can help students persevere in their work until they have done their best. At the same time, teachers should encourage students to be aware of the possibility that sometimes the best thing to do is to start over. For example, if a student chooses a term paper topic but can't find adequate references, the best move may be to simply choose another topic rather than to pursue an unfruitful one.

Language arts (I–C): Teachers can encourage students to recognize that when they are unable to get a creative writing idea to work, they should try another idea and perhaps come back to the original idea at a later time.

Mathematics (HS): Teachers can teach students that, when they take a standardized test, they should not lose too much time on a very difficult math problem and should come back to that problem at the end if there's time.

Science (I–C): Teachers can help students realize what a realistic science project is, given the limitations of available resources.

Social studies (I–C): Teachers can encourage students to switch to another term paper topic if there is insufficient reference material to support their original topic.

Foreign languages (I–C): Teachers can encourage students, when they find a grammatical concept too difficult to understand, to mull it over for a while and come back to it at a later time.

Art (I–C): Teachers can encourage students who are making pottery not to persist if the kiln is causing too many defects.

Music (I–C): Teachers can help students realize that some pieces may be too difficult for them at a given stage of their career, but that they can always come back to playing these pieces when their technique is more advanced.

Physical education (P–HS): Teachers can stress that students should avoid possible danger by not trying to do stretching or lifting exercises after their bodies reach a point of fatigue.

Taking It to Heart

Teachers should list five activities they can assign and discuss with students that will help them differentiate between perseverance and perseveration.

LESSON 24: USE THE RIGHT ABILITIES

Targeted skill: Matching pursuits to abilities

Prompt words or phrases: build on strengths instead of weaknesses, find avenues of excellence, follow paths to success rather than failure

Stumbling block: Using the wrong abilities. Many people become aware, at some time during their lives, that they are either in the wrong occupation or going about that occupation incorrectly. It is as though the work they are doing requires one set of abilities and they are attempting to do it with a different set of abilities.

Using It in Life

Michael Jordan became one of the most successful basketball players of all time. Perhaps because he believed that the challenge was gone, Jordan decided to switch to baseball. He then discovered that his talent for baseball in no way matched his talent for basketball. Jordan then returned to basketball, with great success.

This phenomenon, of course, can occur during schooling as well as in later life. People may find themselves in law school and realize that their cognitive abilities would have been much more suited to an academic career. Or they may find themselves in medical school and come to the conclusion that their real abilities lie in sales. Or they may find that they are brilliant in their area of expertise, but poor in the teaching of that area of expertise. Their discovery, basically, is that they do have strong abilities, but not for the kinds of tasks in which they are engaged. At such a point, the intelligent thing to do is to select another course of schooling or career, or at least switch study or career strategies. Sometimes the "Alices" mentioned in Chapter 3 do not excel as well on the job as they did in school preparing for the job.

Taking It to the Classroom

Teachers should help students recognize person-environment fit. Whether something is creative or useful is determined by the interaction between a person and his or her environment (Csikszentmihalyi, 1988; Gardner, 1993; Sternberg, 2006; Sternberg & Lubart, 1995). A product considered worthwhile in one time or place may be scorned in another.

There is no absolute standard for what constitutes excellent work. The same product or idea may be valued or devalued in different environments. The important thing is either to find a setting in which creative talents and unique contributions are rewarded or to modify the environment.

I once had a student to whom I gave consummately bad advice. This student had two job offers. One was from an institution that was very prestigious but not a good fit for the kind of work she valued. The other institution was a bit less prestigious but much better fit her values. I advised her to take the job in the more prestigious institution, telling her that if she did not accept the job there, she would always wonder what would have happened if she had. Bad advice. She went there and never fit in well. Eventually she left and went to an institution that values her kind of work. Now I always advise students to go for the best fit. It is by developing a constant appreciation of the importance of person-environment fit that students become prepared for choosing environments that are conducive to their creative successes. Teachers can encourage students to examine environments to help them learn to select and match environments with their skills.

Language arts (I–HS): Teachers can encourage students who like to use concise wording to write a haiku poem to express themselves instead of writing a conventional poem.

Mathematics (HS): Teachers can suggest that students write word problems for trigonometry if they like thinking in terms of stories more than in terms of abstract formulas.

Science (C): Teachers can stress to students that to become a medical doctor one needs to excel in the hard science courses required for admission to medical school.

Social studies (P–C): Teachers can give students options on a test, such as allowing them to choose either multiple-choice or essay questions, so that they can choose problems that fit their test taking skills.

Foreign language (I): Teachers can occasionally give students the choice of a written or an oral test.

Art (HS): Teachers can give students a choice of medium for doing an art project.

Music (P–I): Teachers can help students choose a musical instrument that fits their individual skills. (For example, students who have asthma might wish to reflect carefully on whether brass instruments are appropriate for them.)

Physical education (P–HS): Teachers can give students a choice of two sports to play in a physical education class.

Taking It to Heart

Teachers should list five activities they can assign and discuss with students that will help them match their pursuits to their strengths.

LESSON 25: ACT ON A PLAN

Targeted skill: Initiating action

Prompt words or phrases: act, move forward, start, instigate, initiate, just do it

Stumbling block: Inability to translate thought into action. Some people are very adept at coming up with solutions to their problems and may seem to have a solution for every problem in their lives, as well as in the lives of other people, but are unable to translate their thoughts into actions. No matter how good their ideas are, they rarely seem to be able to do anything about them. To capitalize fully on one's intelligence, one must have not only good ideas, but also the ability to do something about these ideas—to translate thought into action. Almost everyone knows of people who have made an important decision for their lives but seem unable to act on it. For example, a couple cannot set a date after deciding to get married. When it comes to action, paralysis sets in. Even though such people may have a high level of intelligence, they are unable to benefit from it. At times, everyone experiences this. The solution is to act rather than to remain buried in thought.

Using It in Life

In interviews with highly successful people, one theme emerges again and again. To the extent that they have regrets, these regrets are rarely over things they have done. Rather, these regrets are almost always over things they have *not* done. They regret lost opportunities. Sometimes people discover that it is "never too late." Both Grigorenko and I were amateur musicians early in our lives, but other things intervened; we never seemed to have enough time to practice, and we both dropped our musical endeavors. While conversing one day, we discovered that we both regretted this, and we made a pact to recommence our musical pursuits. Therefore, after a long lapse, we both decided to correct our mistake not by talk, but by action. I am now happily playing the cello again; Grigorenko, the piano.

Taking It to the Classroom

Teachers can do a number of things to encourage students to develop and implement plans.

Language arts (HS–C): Teachers can encourage students to begin a paper at least a month before it is due rather than wait until the last minute to write it.

Mathematics (P–C): Teachers can encourage students to get started on a difficult math homework assignment early rather than postpone it until they are finished with all their other assignments.

Science (HS): Teachers can encourage students to move forward on a physics experiment by setting out all of the needed materials.

Social studies (P–C): Teachers can help students understand when they have done enough research and should start writing their papers rather than conduct more research.

Foreign language (I–C): Teachers can encourage students to speak the language they are learning whenever possible.

Art (P): Teachers can help students get started on an art project by showing them how to collect materials.

Music (I–HS): Teachers can encourage students not just to think about practicing, but also to do it.

Physical education (HS–C): Teachers can tell students that they can start a new exercise routine by simply showing up at the gym.

Taking It to Heart

Teachers should list five activities they can assign and discuss with students that will help them translate thought into action.

LESSON 26: BECOME ORIENTED TO THE PRODUCT

Targeted skill: Focusing on the end product

Prompt words or phrases: going for the end result, the final product, the outcome

Stumbling block: Lack of product orientation. Some people are very concerned about the process by which things are done but not nearly as concerned about the resulting product. However, accomplishments are judged primarily on the basis of what is produced. Every teacher knows students who have done thorough research, but when it comes to writing it up, they do a second- or third-rate job. Such students are very involved in the research process, but they lose their involvement and enthusiasm when it's time to turn that process into the final product. As a result, their contributions are not considered as important as they could be, and their full level of intelligence does not manifest itself. A similar problem exists with students who have very creative, interesting ideas and may do well in writing an initial draft of a composition but fall short when it comes to polishing the final product.

Using It in Life

Grigorenko once knew a teacher who was dedicated, energetic, and determined. She was willing to do extra research to make her lessons come alive. This social studies teacher would dig through numerous newspapers and magazines to find examples to make her lectures sparkle. However, although she found the research exciting, she found organizing the information and writing a lesson plan boring. As a result, she prepared only half-baked lesson plans. When the time came to teach these lessons to her students, the lessons almost never reached their potential, because she had only the shoddy lesson plans to draw on and couldn't put together all the material on the spot. This teacher's unwillingness to produce the needed product from the research process resulted in her never reaching her full potential as a teacher.

Taking It to the Classroom

Teachers can help students acquire a product-based orientation.

Language arts (I–C): Teachers can encourage students to review a critical essay before handing it in to make sure all important points are thoroughly and clearly expressed.

Mathematics (P–C): Teachers can ask students to review the solutions for all of their homework problems to make sure they make sense.

Science (HS–C): Teachers can encourage students to review each step used to solve a chemistry problem to make sure no errors occurred along the way.

Social studies (HS–C): Teachers can encourage students to prepare and use notes when practicing their speeches for a debate to make sure all the points they want to make are clear and forceful.

Foreign language (I–C): Teachers can ask students to review the rules of verb conjugations when evaluating sentences to make sure the verbs are correctly conjugated.

Art (P): Teachers can ask students to make sure the puppets to be used in a puppet show are prepared for use in the show.

Music (I–C): Teachers can ask students to tape-record a practice session and evaluate their strengths and weakness before giving a solo performance.

Physical education (I–HS): Teachers can encourage students to practice shooting three-pointers during pickup games to prepare for playing against unpredictable basketball opponents.

Taking It to Heart

Teachers should list five activities they can assign and discuss with students that will help them focus on products or goals.

LESSON 27: COMPLETE TASKS

Targeted skill: Finishing what one starts

Prompt words or phrases: complete, finish, close, end, terminate, wrap up, follow through

Stumbling block: Inability to complete tasks and to follow through. The one certain prediction about "noncompleters" is that whatever they begin they will not finish. Nothing in their lives seems to draw quite to a close. Perhaps they are afraid to finish things for fear that they won't know what to do with themselves next. Or they may overwhelm themselves with the details of a project, becoming so hopelessly enmeshed that they are unable to progress. The lives of these people often seem to embody Zeno's paradox. In this paradox, a man wishes to get from point A to point B. In order to traverse the distance, he has to traverse half the distance. In order to traverse the remaining half of the distance, he first has to traverse half of that distance, leaving one quarter of the total distance remaining to be traversed. But in order to traverse that distance, he first has to complete half of that. In the paradox, the man always goes half of the remaining distance, and never arrives. Similarly, some people seem unable to reach the ends of situations or projects.

Using It in Life

Lifelong learning is an important skill for any person to acquire. But there is a difference between being a lifelong learner and being a perpetual student. Perpetual students start one thing after another but never seem to complete anything they start. Often their lives are littered with the detritus of innumerable false starts. There can be multiple reasons that a person is a noncompleter. Some people are afraid to take responsibility for declaring something done. Others fear that after they are done with a program of work they will not know how to move on. But people need to be able to wrap up phases of their work or even of their lives, and then to go forward from there.

Taking It to the Classroom

Teachers and students alike need to know when the time has come to wrap things up. Teachers need to wrap up lessons, and students need to wrap up their learning of lessons.

Language arts (I–HS): Teachers can help students end a poem by encouraging them to end it at the last stanza they feel proud of.

Mathematics (HS–C): Teachers can help students recognize when they need to end a calculus practice session in order to get a good night's sleep before an exam.

Science (I–C): Teachers can ask students to terminate a log of observations of cross-pollination after three generations instead of eight, if three generations display enough information for a report.

Social studies (HS–C): Teachers can ask students to recognize when it's time to wrap up their work on a term paper the night before the paper is due, even if the paper is not as thorough as they would like it to be.

Foreign language (I–C): Teachers can encourage students to make sure they allow enough time to memorize a list of words before a test.

Art (P): Teachers can ask students to know when to finish a drawing so that they can proceed to their next activity.

Music (P–C): Teachers can encourage students to end piano practice when their fingers start to ache.

Physical education (P–HS): Teachers can help students realize when they should wrap up sprint practice, even if they didn't reach their best time.

Taking It to Heart

Teachers should list five activities they can assign and discuss with students that will help them develop the habit of completing what they start.

LESSON 28: MAKE A COMMITMENT

Targeted skill: Initiating projects and committing oneself to a goal

Prompt words or phrases: commit, choose, begin, initiate

Stumbling block: Failure to initiate projects. Some people seem unwilling or unable to commit to or to initiate projects; they are always trying to decide what to do. Often this inability to initiate results from fear of commitment. Certain people are afraid to become too committed to anything, and, as a result, they are unable to undertake anything.

Using It in Life

Being unable to commit often causes people to leave projects or undertakings unfinished. Some students fail to complete graduate school because they never commit themselves to a dissertation topic. A dissertation requires a substantial investment of time and energy, and some students are simply unwilling to make this commitment.

Many people act this way in interpersonal relationships. They never seem to want to go beyond initially meeting people for fear of becoming committed to a relationship. As a result, they go through life in a series of superficial relationships, unable to initiate a more substantial relationship that runs the risk of leading to a commitment.

Taking It to the Classroom

Teachers can encourage students to research possible topics for projects and then to commit to one of these topics. It is important that students learn to research the possibilities, but students also need to learn to commit to one of the many options that arise.

Language arts (I–C): Teachers can encourage students to choose a favorite modern author to write about and start writing.

Mathematics (HS): Teachers can ask students to commit to completing a particular geometry project.

Science (P): Teachers can ask students to decide which of two science exploration activities to do when both are offered simultaneously.

Social studies (I–HS): Teachers can encourage students to select a side to support in a debate on local community-based policing.

Foreign language (I–C): Teachers can encourage students to choose a country to visit for student exchange as part of the foreign language program.

Art (P): Teachers can ask students to choose a medium to work in for an art session.

Music (I–C): Teachers can ask students to commit to a piece of music to perform.

Physical education (HS–C): Teachers can ask students to determine their choice of a swimming stroke to use in competition.

Taking It to Heart

Teachers should list five activities they can assign and discuss with students that will help them practice committing to a project.

LESSON 29: TAKE A RISK

Targeted skill: Controlling fear of failure

Prompt words or phrases: take a risk, venture, dare, trust

Stumbling block: Fear of failure. Fear of failure seems to start early in life. This problem is very common, especially in individuals at the extremes of the continuum in achievement. Low achievers may fear failure because they have experienced too much of it; high achievers may fear failure because they have not learned to accept occasional failures as a normal part of learning.

Using It in Life

Many people fail to realize their full intellectual potential because they fear they will fail at what they do. In college, they may not take the difficult courses they need because they don't expect to do well in them. As a result, they may do well in the courses they take but later have no use for that material and discover that they need the content from the courses they avoided. Later on, as lawyers, doctors, scientists, or business executives, they may not undertake the projects that could really make a difference to their careers because they fear that the projects will not succeed. Indeed, they may not even enter their desired occupation because they fear they will not succeed in it. In other cases, they may not continue with a personal relationship, not because of the way it is going, but rather because of the way it might go.

In some cases, fear of failure may be realistic. If the consequences of failure are high enough, fear of failure can be quite adaptive. For example, the whole strategy of nuclear deterrence depends on fear of failure—the theory being that no country will start a nuclear war due to the fear that it will be a disaster for them as well as for their opponents. Thus, there are times at which it is quite reasonable not to take risks. But there are other times when a person must take risks, and the unwillingness or inability to do so results in loss of opportunities that may never return.

Taking It to the Classroom

Teachers should allow students to make mistakes, as buying low and selling high carries a risk. Many ideas are unpopular simply because they are not good; people often think a certain way because that way works better than other ways. But once in a while, a great thinker comes along—a Freud, a Piaget, a Chomsky, or an Einstein—and demonstrates a new way to think. These thinkers contributed successfully because they allowed themselves and their collaborators to take risks and make mistakes. For example, many of Freud's and Piaget's ideas are wrong. Freud confused Victorian issues regarding sexuality with universal conflicts and Piaget misjudged the ages at which children can perform certain cognitive feats. Their ideas were great not because they lasted forever, but because they became the basis for other ideas. Freud's and Piaget's mistakes allowed others to profit from and go beyond the earlier ideas. Both of these scientists learned from their mistakes.

Schools are often unforgiving of mistakes. Errors in schoolwork are usually marked with a large X. If students respond to questions with incorrect answers, some teachers pounce on the students for not having read or understood the material, while classmates may snicker. In hundreds of ways and in thousands of instances over the course of a school career, students learn that it is not all right to make mistakes. The result is that they become afraid to risk the independent and sometimes flawed thinking that leads to creativity.

When students make mistakes, teachers should ask them to analyze and discuss these mistakes. Often, mistakes or weak ideas contain the germ of correct answers or good ideas. In Japan, teachers spend entire class periods asking students to analyze the mistakes in their mathematical thinking (e.g., Stevenson & Stigler, 1994). For teachers who want to make a difference, exploring mistakes can be an opportunity for learning and growing.

> **Language arts (P–C):** Teachers can ask students to write a story with an unconventional ending, such as one in which a conflict is left unresolved or the hero dies.
>
> **Mathematics (P–C):** Teachers can encourage students to attempt to solve a really hard problem on a practice test that will be graded.
>
> **Science (I–HS):** Teachers can ask students to suggest activities they would like to do, even if they're not totally sure they can succeed in them.
>
> **Social studies (I–HS):** Teachers can ask students to defend the losers of a major war.
>
> **Foreign language (HS–C):** Teachers can encourage students to talk in a foreign language to native speakers of that language, even if they do not know the language well.
>
> **Art (P–C):** Teachers can ask students to make unusual clay objects instead of the usual bowls or pencil holders.
>
> **Music (I):** Teachers can encourage students to choose to play a new instrument in addition to an instrument they have played before.
>
> **Physical education (I–HS):** Teachers can encourage students to try out for the softball team even if they don't think they will make it.

Taking It to Heart

Teachers should list five activities they can assign and discuss with students that will help them learn how to handle a failure and thus overcome fear of failing.

LESSON 30: DON'T PROCRASTINATE

Targeted skill: Overcoming procrastination

Prompt words or phrases: start, take the first step, begin, do it today

Stumbling block: Procrastination. Procrastination seems to be a universal fact of life. Everyone, at some time or another, procrastinates, putting off until later the things they know should be done now. Procrastination becomes a serious problem only when it is a person's uniform strategy for doing things. In any career or stage of life, it is easy for people to become immersed in the daily trivia that can gobble up all of their time. The tendency to become so immersed may actually result in short-term success, but it often results in long-term failure. Those with a tendency toward procrastination often have to force themselves to undertake the big things because they are simply unable to do them without pressure, whether self-imposed or imposed by others.

Using It in Life

Some students tend to look for little things to do to put off the big things. They always manage to get their daily reading and assignments done, but they seem to procrastinate forever in undertaking the large-scale projects that can really make a difference in their academic careers. Similarly, some younger students do well in day-to-day classroom work but procrastinate when it comes to studying for exams or writing papers, and therefore they end up with grades that don't reflect their actual abilities.

Taking It to the Classroom

Teachers can encourage students to get started on long-term projects rather than procrastinate. One way teachers can do this is by requiring students to set subgoals. For example, if the long-term goal is an independent project, teachers can have students write proposals, prepare detailed outlines, and hand in rough drafts before the final due date for the project.

Language arts (I): Teachers can ask students to set daily goals for completing specific parts of the book *Tom Sawyer.*

Mathematics (I–C): Teachers can encourage students to review several extra practice problems every day to prepare for a final exam.

Science (P–C): Teachers can encourage students to begin a research project by going to the library immediately.

Social studies (HS–C): Teachers can encourage students to take the first step in reporting on the relationship between NATO and Eastern Europe by starting to search online for news immediately.

Foreign language (I–C): Teachers can request that students practice using words from the weekly vocabulary list by using them in sentences daily.

Art (HS–C): Teachers can ask students to begin a portrait by making a grid and aiming to complete a specific number of squares per day.

Music (P): Teachers can encourage students to each sing a song each day before the class will sing it as a group.

Physical education (I–C): Teachers can encourage students to immediately start a special dietary program that will improve their performance.

Taking It to Heart

Teachers should list five activities they can assign and discuss with students that will help them overcome procrastination.

LESSON 31: ASSIGN RESPONSIBILITY

Targeted skill: Attributing credit or blame for results to whom it belongs

Prompt words or phrases: accept responsibility, assess contribution, admit failure or success, weigh contribution

Stumbling block: Misattribution of blame. Some people feel they can do no wrong and are always looking for others to blame for even the slightest mishap. Other people are always blaming themselves for everything, regardless of their role in the event or events that led to a mishap or a success. Misattribution of blame or responsibility seriously hinders a person's intellectual self-realization and closes the door to self-improvement.

Using It in Life

I once worked with a graduate student who was very able and competent in research. The faculty thought the world of this student, and yet she always blamed herself for anything that went wrong. It reached the point where she felt that she could do nothing right, and she seemed traumatized much of the time. Eventually, this student left the program.

Another graduate student was exactly the opposite. This student always managed to blame others for things that went wrong in his graduate career. Although it was clear to practically everyone surrounding him that he just was not working very hard, he always had an excuse for why things were not getting done. These excuses tended to involve the machinations of others, which he claimed prevented him from working toward and reaching his goals. He never achieved much success and never accepted responsibility for what he viewed as bad luck.

Taking It to the Classroom

Part of teaching students to be effective in their work is teaching them to take responsibility for both successes and failures. Teaching students how to take responsibility means teaching students to (a) understand their thinking processes, (b) critique themselves, and (c) take pride in their best work. Unfortunately, many teachers and parents look for, or allow students to look for, an outside enemy to be held responsible for failures.

It sounds trite to recommend that teachers teach students to take responsibility for themselves, but sometimes there is a gap between the known and how to translate the known into action. In practice, people differ widely in the extent to which they take responsibility, whether in the form of credit or blame, for the causes and consequences of their actions. Effective people need to take responsibility for themselves and for their ideas while not blaming themselves for consequences that are not their responsibility.

Language arts (P–I): Teachers can encourage students to accept responsibility for not doing well on a reading test when they had not been paying attention to the teacher.

Mathematics (I–C): Teachers can encourage students to admit that they failed a test because they had not studied the correct material.

Science (I-C): Teachers can ask students to each assess their contribution to their lab group's failure to complete the target chemical synthesis.

Social studies (I–HS): Teachers can ask students to weigh the contributions that their ill-thought-out perspectives about UN policy made to the class discussion before they question the mediocre grades given them for the discussion.

Foreign language (I–C): Teachers can encourage students to admit that their failure to pronounce certain foreign words correctly was the source of their low grades on a speaking facility test.

Art (P–C): Teachers can ask students to assess how well they followed directions for a craft project that fell apart soon after they brought it home.

Music (I–C): Teachers can encourage students to accept responsibility for poor progress in violin class because they have not practiced in the past week.

Physical education (HS): Teachers can ask students to admit failure to jump to a target height and encourage them to move on to another activity when jumping practice is taking too much of their time.

Taking It to Heart

Teachers should list five activities they can assign and discuss with students that will help them learn how to accept both credit and blame when earned.

LESSON 32: MANAGE SELF-PITY

Targeted skill: Moving on

Prompt words or phrases: take stock, pull oneself together, get on with it

Stumbling block: Excessive self-pity. All people pity themselves sometimes. When things don't go just right, it's difficult not to. But constant self-pity is highly maladaptive. Self-pity is not only useless for getting work done, but it also, after a certain point, tends to put off those who might otherwise be most helpful.

Using It in Life

A student entered a graduate program with certain clear disadvantages in terms of preparation, and he felt sorry for himself. At that point others felt sorry for him too. But after a while, people became annoyed and even angry at his continual self-pity. After a point, he was expected to pull himself up by his boot-straps and make a go of things. But his self-pity never seemed to end. A vicious circle ensued—as he became sorrier and sorrier for himself, others became less and less sorry, until finally they wanted to have little to do with him. He seemed to spend more time feeling sorry for himself than making the effort that would allow him to no longer have any cause to feel sorry.

Taking It to the Classroom

In contrast, Stephen Hawking is one of the more physically disabled individuals in the world. He suffers from a debilitating, progressive disease. He might have spent his time feeling sorry for himself. Instead, he has spent his time becoming one of the leading astrophysicists of his generation.

Language arts (P): Teachers can encourage their students to not let the embarrassment of mispronouncing a word stop them from speaking up in class.

Mathematics (I–HS): Teachers can encourage students to pull themselves together after getting a low grade for a math project they had spent a lot of time completing.

Science (HS–C): Teachers can encourage students to move on to the next section of an anatomy assignment, even if at the moment they can't seem to remember all of the organs of the system they reviewed earlier in the day.

Social studies (P–C): Teachers can ask students to take stock of what they didn't understand on a U.S. history test and resolve to learn that part better for the final exam.

Foreign language (HS–C): Teachers can encourage students to pull themselves together when they feel humiliated because they communicated poorly to a person who fluently speaks a foreign language.

Art (I–C): Teachers can encourage students to move on to another project when their ceramic pitcher cracks in the kiln.

Music (P–C): Teachers can ask students to take stock of how lack of technique negatively affected their performance and resolve to concentrate on strengthening those weaknesses to give a better performance in the future.

Physical education (P–HS): Teachers can encourage students to get on with a bicycle race after they have fallen.

Taking It to Heart

Teachers should list five activities they can assign and discuss with students that will help them recognize and work on overcoming excessive self-pity.

LESSON 33: BE INDEPENDENT

Targeted skill: Developing independence

Prompt words or phrases: developing maturity, standing on one's own, becoming self-reliant, being self-starting

Stumbling Block: Excessive dependency. If a person wants something done, it is best for her to either do it herself or take responsibility for having another do it. Generally, people expect individuals to be responsible for tasks or actions that are accepted behavior for persons of their age. A sign of independence is being able to perform those parts of a task that are clearly a personal responsibility in a timely and autonomous manner.

Using It in Life

How can teachers predict which students will be successful, not only in the classroom, but also in the world at large? Grigorenko and I used to look for ability and motivation, both of which, of course, are important. We have found, however, that independence is equally important. Many individuals make good students: they do what they're told. But they may not be able to make the transition to being successful on their own. It is therefore important for teachers to nurture not only excellence in their students, but also excellence when students are working independently.

I once had a student who was a wonderful teaching assistant. He did exactly what he was told and did it well. Therefore, it was a surprise that when this individual took a job, he was not a successful teacher at all. He had been a great student teacher, but he was unable to function effectively when teaching independently.

Taking It to the Classroom

Students are expected to acquire a certain degree of independence in most of the tasks they face. Even in the early elementary grades, students are usually expected to gradually assume some independence—to remember to bring papers home, to work independently in the classroom, to complete homework on time, and so on. The inability to be independent in age-appropriate ways can seriously compromise a student's chances of school success.

Often people's home lives ill prepare them for the independence that later will be expected of them. To some extent in school, and especially after they enter a career, people are expected to fend for themselves and to rely upon others only to the minimal degree necessary. Many students seem not to learn this, and they expect others either to do things for them or to constantly show them how to get things done. Without such aid, they are at a total loss.

The result is that they often have to seek less responsible jobs, or that they never do as well as they otherwise might in the job that they have.

Language arts (I–C): Teachers can encourage students to look up examples of good short stories that they would like to model their short story after instead of asking the teacher what to do.

Mathematics (I–HS): Teachers can ask students to show self-reliance by completing extra practice problems and practice exams before deciding to request a tutor.

Science (P–I): Teachers can encourage students to self-start their review process for their class on the human body by drawing colorful diagrams of various bodily processes.

Social studies (HS–C): Teachers can ask students to review the possible options for a research paper several weeks in advance in order to ask informed questions about the assignment.

Foreign language (I–C): Teachers can encourage students to participate in a conversational class (so that the teacher can correct their mistakes in class) rather than wait to ask questions (or make mistakes because they did not ask questions) until later.

Art (I–HS): Teachers can ask students to show maturity in composition class by finding their own examples of artwork to use for models instead of asking the teacher for ideas.

Music (I–C): Teachers can encourage students to display self-reliance by listening to great performers play the piece they are learning in order to understand how it should be played instead of waiting for the teacher to show or tell them.

Physical education (P–I): Teachers can encourage students to express initiative by training on their own to improve their strength for a gymnastics performance rather than waiting for the instructor to tell them what they need to do to increase their strength.

Taking It to Heart

Teachers should list five activities they can assign and discuss with students that will help them develop appropriate independence.

LESSON 34: HANDLE PERSONAL DIFFICULTIES

Targeted skill: Surmounting personal problems

Prompt words or phrases: keep in perspective, work through, overcome, despite, carry on, develop resilience

Stumbling block: Wallowing in personal difficulties. Everyone has personal difficulties, but their extent differs widely from one person to another. Some people have repeated tragedies in their lives, whereas others seem to lead charmed existences and almost never encounter difficulties. During the course of life, people can expect some real joys, but also some real sorrows. It is important that individuals try to keep both the joys and the sorrows in perspective; in fact, people can choose to be or not to be overwhelmed and thrown into disarray by a personal problem. Some people let their personal difficulties interfere grossly with their work; others seem to be unaffected in their work and carry on in spite of a major disruption. Major life crises almost always have some effect on a person's work, whether he or she likes it or not. People need to accept that this will happen and take it in stride. It is equally important that people not wallow in their personal difficulties and let those difficulties drag down their work and themselves. Indeed, in times of personal hardship, a person's work, as well as other people, may provide him or her with some needed solace. It is a mistake for people to avoid the personal difficulties they must often face, and it is equally a mistake for them to allow themselves to be consumed by such difficulties.

Using It in Life

Students come from diverse backgrounds and face diverse family problems as well as other problems. The same, of course, is true of teachers. At some point or another, almost everyone faces serious challenges in his or her personal life. The issue is not whether such challenges will arise; they will. The issue is how people get through these issues. Will a death, a divorce, a health problem, or a financial problem bring them down? Or will they face such challenges with determination and then have the resilience to bounce back? It is almost always in a person's control to bounce back. The question is whether people choose to master their lives or to be mastered by them.

Taking It to the Classroom

Students need to be given examples of people who faced enormous challenges and bounced back. Martin Luther King, Jr., faced stiff opposition from racists but did not let their opposition get to him. The great president Abraham Lincoln came from a modest background. Nelson Mandela was jailed for much of his life, but he went on to become a leader of and hero to not only South Africa, but also the entire world.

Language arts (P–C): Teachers can encourage students to use a personal tragedy, such as the loss of a pet or close friend, as motivation for writing about sorrow or friendship.

Mathematics (P–C): Teachers can remind students that although school seems to be highly frustrating at times, neglecting assignments will only add to their stress level later on.

Science (I–C): Teachers can encourage students to work through a tragedy by finding solace in the observation of nature.

Social studies (P–HS): Teachers can ask students to share their perspective on drunk driving if they or a loved one have suffered in an alcohol-related car crash.

Foreign language (I–C): Teachers can encourage students to carry on despite a personal tragedy by writing about how people in other cultures express their feelings of turmoil and how they deal with those feelings.

Art (I–C): Teachers can encourage students to work through strained personal situations by using color and media that express their emotional states.

Music (I–C): Teachers can ask students to play joyful music in their orchestra, despite their negative emotions, to make themselves feel better.

Physical education (P–C): Teachers can ask students to try to separate their personal problems from their physical performance by focusing on the goal of scoring points for their team.

Taking It to Heart

Teachers should list five activities they can assign and discuss with students that will help them recognize and overcome the effects of personal difficulties.

LESSON 35: CONCENTRATE

Targeted skill: Concentrating

Prompt words or phrases: concentrate, attend to, focus, heed, center in on, be engrossed in

Stumbling block: Distractibility and lack of concentration. There are any number of very intelligent people who, despite their high intelligence, never seem to be able to concentrate on anything for very long. They are highly distractible and tend to have short attention spans. As a result, they don't get much done. To some extent, distractibility is an attention variable over which a person does not have total control. If an individual has good concentration, then this stumbling block is not a worry. But many people are distractible and have difficulty concentrating. These people need to structure their working environment to minimize distractions. In effect, they need to create an environment in which they can concentrate. If they don't, they will have difficulty reaching their goals.

Using It in Life

Several months ago, I went to a concert given by a cello soloist. Halfway through the concert something went wrong with the hearing aid of a gentleman in the audience. The hearing aid started emitting a loud, high-pitched noise. Many people in the audience found themselves distracted, their concentration broken. Amazingly, the soloist did not skip a beat. He continued playing the music flawlessly, as though nothing out of the ordinary was happening. After the concert, I had the opportunity to speak with him and I asked him how he could continue to play. He replied that what distinguishes the true professional in any field is not just his best performance, but his ability to perform optimally under any conditions. In the concert, he showed that he had the ability to give his best, regardless of any distraction that might come his way. Of course, there are limits. It is said that the musicians on the *Titanic* continued to play even as the ship was sinking!

Taking It to the Classroom

Teachers can help students who are unusually distractible by providing them with an appropriate work environment and by encouraging them to create such an environment for themselves (e.g., by finding a quiet place in which to do homework). Students differ in how they react to background sounds. Some work better while listening to music, while others lose their concentration. Students need to learn what level and type of ambient noise works for them.

Language arts (P–C): Teachers can ask students to choose to memorize their lines for a dramatic play in an empty auditorium instead of in their room at home in order to have more peace and quiet.

Mathematics (P–C): Teachers can tell students that when they feel unmotivated, they should work on math problems with another person and compare answers instead of working by themselves.

Science (P–C): Teachers can suggest that students read the dense textbook for science class at the library instead of in their living rooms with the television on.

Social studies (HS–C): Teachers can ask students to concentrate on the topic of their thesis (e.g., euthanasia) instead of becoming distracted by related issues (e.g., the quality of health care in the United States).

Foreign language (I–C): Teachers can encourage students to review conversational exercises with headphones instead of with a stereo so others are less likely to interrupt them.

Art (P–HS): Teachers can suggest that students find an environment that stimulates many artistic ideas, such as a town park.

Music (P–C): Teachers can encourage students to set aside a specific time and practice room every day to ensure that they stick to a practice routine.

Physical education (P–C): Teachers can encourage students to train when the gym is relatively empty so that they are not distracted by socializing.

Taking It to Heart

Teachers should list five activities they can assign and discuss with students that will help them avoid distractions and focus on the problem at hand.

LESSON 36: SCHEDULE ACCORDINGLY

Targeted skill: Distributing activities sensibly

Prompt words or phrases: apportion, divide, plan, schedule, just say no, prioritize

Stumbling Block: Spreading oneself too thin or too thick. People who spread themselves too thin sometimes find that they can get nothing done, not because they don't work hard enough, but because their progress is small on each of the large number of projects they are pursuing. People with this tendency need to recognize this inclination within themselves and to counteract it as necessary. If they undertake multiple projects, they must try to stagger or arrange their projects so that they have a reasonable probability of finishing each of them in an acceptable amount of time.

Other people find themselves unable to undertake more than one or two things at a given time. This disposition is fine as long as people progress through their activities with reasonable dispatch. When people undertake too little at one time, they can miss opportunities and their level of accomplishment can be reduced.

People need to find the right distribution of activities for themselves and then maximize their performance within that distribution. They need to avoid undertaking either more or less than they can handle at a single time.

Using It in Life

Grigorenko and I knew a teacher who seemed unable to say no. She wanted to please everyone. If a student wanted her to be an adviser, she said yes. If asked by the chairperson to teach an extra course, she said yes. If asked to be on a committee, she said yes. Finally, this helpful, dedicated individual came up for tenure. She was denied. Why? She was told she had spread herself too thin. In trying to do so many things for so many people, she had neglected to get done those things that most needed to get done, such as keeping up with her research. By spreading herself too thin, she ended up pleasing neither the department nor herself. She, too, was disappointed in how little of her own agenda she had accomplished.

Taking It to the Classroom

Students need to get a sense of what constitutes a reasonable distribution of commitments for them. They need to decide how many extracurricular activities they can do without compromising their academic work, and which activities are really important to them and which can go. If they don't learn to deal with this issue as students, they may end up paying the price for the rest of their lives.

Language arts (HS): Teachers can encourage students to avoid extra English club activities when they are already involved in a poetry group and a book club as well as being full-time students.

Mathematics (I–C): Teachers can encourage students to schedule enough time to read assigned material, complete homework, and check their answers.

Science (C): Teachers can ask students to plan how they can take an advanced chemistry class, instruct the laboratory sessions for an introductory chemistry class, fulfill the requirements for their other courses, and still have time to relax.

Social studies (P–C): Teachers can encourage students to set priorities for the clubs they are interested in joining and then participate in only a small number of organizations so they can be actively involved in each of them.

Foreign language (HS–C): Teachers can ask students to evaluate whether they can afford to take a year off from their school's curriculum before they decide to become a foreign exchange student.

Art (HS–C): Teachers can encourage students to determine the amount of money they can spend on each project before buying the supplies so they can be sure they can complete all the projects.

Music (I–C): Teachers can suggest that students decide how much time they should spend practicing each part of a demanding musical challenge to be ready to present their progress to their teacher in a week.

Physical education (P–C): Teachers can encourage students to set priorities for athletic involvement so they can decide which sports they want to spend their time on.

Taking It to Heart

Teachers should list five activities they can assign and discuss with students that will help them learn to identify and schedule reasonable time to carry out their activities.

LESSON 37: SET PRIORITIES

Targeted skill: Keeping the goal in view

Prompt words or phrases: set priorities, see the big picture, keep your eye on the goal

Stumbling block: Inability or unwillingness to see the forest for the trees. Everyone has known people who are intellectually very capable but relatively unsuccessful in their careers because they can't see the forest for the trees. That is, they obsess over small details and are unwilling or unable to see or to deal with the larger picture in the projects they undertake. These people become so absorbed with the microstructure of whatever they undertake that they ignore or pay only minimal attention to the macrostructure. For example, some teachers become so bogged down in the everyday demands of planning individual lessons, correcting papers, and so on, that they lose sight of their broader goals.

Using It in Life

There are times when minutiae are important. For example, in designing computers, spacecraft, or cars, even the most minor slips can have major repercussions when the product malfunctions. However, in many aspects of life, it is necessary to concentrate on the big picture, or at least never to lose sight of it. Over the years, Grigorenko and I have observed large numbers of students who ended up pursuing careers that left them bored, disappointed, or both. There are many reasons for such unfortunate career decisions, but one of them is a failure to consider the big picture. Sometimes students chose a career simply because it was what their parents wanted for them. Other times they went for the money and little else. Still other times they started down a career path and just never stepped back and asked themselves whether the path they had chosen was the right one for them. The common element is a failure to look at the whole forest instead of looking at just a few trees.

Taking It to the Classroom

It is very easy for students to become so bogged down in the day-to-day details of student life that they lose sight of the big picture. If this happens, they need to set aside time to think about the larger issues. During those times, they should concentrate on the meaning of what they're doing and where they wish to go. Without such time, students may find themselves losing track not only of how what they are doing will help them reach their goals, but also of what those goals originally were.

Language arts (P–C): Teachers can encourage students to try to understand the message an author is trying to convey, not just the details of the author's writing.

Mathematics (P–C): Teachers can help students recognize not just how to execute a particular mathematical algorithm, but also when to use it.

Science (HS–C): Teachers can help students understand that a good grasp of physics really will help them when they enter an engineering competition to build the fastest race car.

Social studies (P–C): Teachers can encourage students to realize that past events can help them understand current events and even predict future events.

Foreign language (I–C): Teachers can help students realize that their vocabulary words may someday help them speak to someone with whom they otherwise would not be able to communicate.

Art (I–C): Teachers can ask students to accept that basic drawing techniques may be boring to practice but will help them to draw more accurately, to paint more proportionally, and to convey important characteristics more effectively.

Music (P–C): Teachers can encourage students to realize that practicing scales may be boring but is essential for developing technique.

Physical education (I–C): Teachers can suggest that students keep in mind that small details such as breathing rhythm can affect their overall performance in competitions.

Taking It to Heart

Teachers should list five activities they can assign and discuss with students that will help them avoid getting bogged down in small details and concentrate on goals.

LESSON 38: BALANCE THINKING SKILLS

Targeted skill: Balancing analytical, creative, and practical abilities

Prompt words or phrases: balance, judge, equalize, adjust

Stumbling block: Lack of balance among analytical, creative, and practical thinking. There are times in life when individuals need to be critical and analytical; there are other times when they need to be creative and synthetic; and there are still other times when they need to apply thinking in practice. It is important for individuals to know which times are which.

Using It in Life

I visited Hong Kong a few years ago and spoke to teachers at the National Institute of Education about creativity. One teacher in the audience looked puzzled. Why, she wondered, was I speaking about creativity when teaching is not a creative occupation?

On the contrary, the authors of this book believe that all highly successful teachers balance analytical, creative, and practical skills. Analytical skill is needed to figure out which teaching techniques are succeeding and which are not. They need creative skill to come up with new lesson plans and to keep their teaching fresh and flexible. Flexibility is a key to success in an age in which knowledge, technology, and even social customs are rapidly changing. And teachers need practical ability to find just the right way to reach their students—to teach them at just the right level and in just the right way. Triarchic thinking is not just a story about learning; it is a story about teaching, too.

Taking It to the Classroom

Some students frequently seem to make the wrong judgments about their classroom interactions. They complain bitterly that their teachers fail to recognize their creativity on objective, multiple-choice tests, or they complain that their teachers don't give them credit for how well organized, if uninspired, their papers are. Although these students may have good analytical and creative abilities, they don't know when to apply which abilities.

It's important that individuals learn what kind of thinking is expected of a person in different kinds of situations, and then to try to do the kind of thinking that is appropriate for the given situation. For example, standardized multiple-choice mental ability tests don't usually provide good opportunities to demonstrate creativity, unless they are explicitly designed to measure creativity. Research projects, on the other hand, are excellent opportunities to show creativity. The point is that it is important for individuals not only to have analytical, creative, and practical abilities, but also to know when to use them. Ideally, teachers should teach students to balance the kinds of thinking illustrated by Alice, Barbara, and Celia in Chapter 3.

Language arts (HS–C): Teachers can help students recognize that an essay question about the characters in a specific book requires analytical ability (for correctly identifying the characters and their traits), practical ability (for showing how the characters are realistic), and creative ability (for discovering and writing about one's unique perspective on the book).

Mathematics (HS): Teachers can help students realize that textbook trigonometry problems require mostly analytical ability.

Science (I–C): Teachers can help students understand that lab experiments require analytical ability (for identifying the components of the experiment correctly), creative ability (for generating good ideas for the experiments), and practical ability (for precisely following directions and applying learning to the real world).

Social studies (I–C): Teachers can help students realize that research papers allow room for creativity if students can analytically and practically support their creative perspective.

Foreign language (P–C): Teachers can help students recognize that it is practical to learn a specific foreign language if they need to communicate regularly with people who speak primarily that language.

Art (P–C): Teachers can help students understand that art requires creative ability (for generating ideas for compositions), analytical ability (for considering technique), and practical ability (for making the artwork appealing to others).

Music (HS–C): Teachers can help students recognize that the practicality of composing music depends on who the intended audience is.

Physical education (I–C): Teachers can help students realize that sports require creative ability, especially when two opposing teams are equally matched, and that a novel move by a player could result in her team's winning the game.

Taking It to Heart

Teachers should list five activities they can assign and discuss with students that will help them recognize appropriate times to use each of the three thinking skills.

LESSON 39: DEVELOP SELF-CONFIDENCE

Targeted skill: Developing realistic self-confidence

Prompt words or phrases: reviewing and assessing, balancing pride and humility

Stumbling block: Too little or too much self-confidence. Everyone needs a hefty measure of self-confidence to get through life. There can be so many blows to individuals' self-esteem and views of themselves that without self-confidence they are at the mercy of all the minor and major setbacks that continually confront them. Lack of self-confidence seems to gnaw away at some people's ability to get things done well, because they actually seem to realize their own self-doubts in their work. These self-doubts become self-fulfilling prophecies. Self-confidence is often essential for success. After all, if people don't have confidence in themselves, how can they expect others to have confidence in them?

At the same time, it is important for individuals not to have too much or misplaced self-confidence. As many students fail due to excessive self-confidence as students who fail due to too little. Individuals with too much self-confidence don't know when to admit they are wrong or in need of self-improvement. As a result, they rarely improve as rapidly as they are able.

Using It in Life

Too little or too much self-confidence can be especially damaging in job interviews. Applicants with too little self-confidence fail to inspire the confidence of those who might employ them. Their lack of self-confidence transfers to the potential employer, who also ends up not having confidence in them. Too much self-confidence can put people off and lead to resentment and the desire to strike back—to tell the individual in some way that he or she is not as great as he or she thinks. Unfortunately, this striking back can occur in the form of a decision not to hire a person.

Another example of this problem relates to student teaching. Student teachers with low self-confidence tend to have trouble commanding respect from their students. At the same time, those who are too confident may turn off the cooperating teacher or may not recognize that they still have much to learn. It is important that individuals strike just the right balance between too little and too much of a good thing.

Taking It to the Classroom

One of the best gifts teachers can give students is meaningful self-confidence. In other words, students' self-confidence should be high enough to encourage them to seek challenges, but not so high that they believe they have nothing left to learn.

Language arts (P–HS): Teachers can suggest that students build their confidence enough to try out for a demanding role in the school play.

Mathematics (P–C): Teachers can ask students to maintain humility when they get the top score in the class by helping others understand the harder problems.

Science (HS–C): Teachers can ask students to assess whether they were too hasty in their guess at the answer on a test because they felt overly confident.

Social studies (P–C): Teachers can encourage students to display confidence when they present their case in a class discussion.

Foreign language (I–C): Teachers can encourage students to show confidence by attempting to enter into a conversation in a foreign language.

Art (I–C): Teachers can ask students to determine whether their pottery project displays their potential and to be humble about their success if they feel that they reached their ideal.

Music (P–C): Teachers can encourage students to build their confidence to enter into musical competitions.

Physical education (P–C): Teachers can suggest that students show self-confidence on the tennis court and not always blame their partner when their team loses.

Taking It to Heart

Teachers should list five activities they can assign and discuss with students that will help them develop self-confidence that reflects their strengths and acknowledges their weaknesses.

LESSON 40: ADDITIONAL PROMPTS FOR PRACTICAL THINKING

Targeted skill: Thinking practically

Prompt words or phrases: use, employ, apply, put into practice, implement

Nineteen potential stumbling blocks to the realization of intellectual potential have been described as lessons in practical thinking. This material may seem only vaguely related to the topic of the book—teaching for thinking—or it may even seem moralistic. However, it is easy for those who wish to understand and develop the intellect to become buried in thought. Individuals must never lose sight of the fact that what really matters in the world is not the level of a person's intelligence, but rather what he achieves with this intelligence. An individual's ultimate goal in understanding and increasing intelligence should be the full realization in life of the intellectual potential within himself.

Here are some additional prompts that can be used in teaching for practical thinking:

Language Arts

- Teachers can have students use the same techniques Tom Sawyer used to convince his friends to whitewash Aunt Polly's fence to convince someone to buy something from them.
- Teachers can ask students how they can employ what they learned from reading *Hatchet* if they find themselves alone in a wilderness area.
- Teachers can have students show how they could apply one lesson they learned from *Love in the Time of Cholera* to improve their relationships with loved ones.

Mathematics

- Teachers can ask students to use what they have learned about percentages to describe how store owners figure out their profits on the sale of a piece of merchandise.
- Teachers can ask students how trigonometry is employed in the building of bridges.
- Teachers can encourage students to show how they could apply multiplication of fractions to modify a recipe for a smaller number of people.
- Teachers can have students run a simulated bank in their classroom.

Science

- Teachers can suggest that students use what they know about photosynthesis to discuss why plant life is essential for the world's oxygen supply.

- Teachers can ask students how scientists have employed what they know about the reproduction of bacteria to create certain kinds of antibiotics.
- Teachers can encourage students to apply what they have learned about the relationship between correlation and causation to show that a correlation between the amount of food eaten and good health does not imply that eating a large amount of food causes good health.
- Teachers can have students imagine what it would be like to live on a planet with much less gravity than the planet earth.

Social Studies

- Teachers can tell students to use the war in Iraq as an example for describing why it is important that a nation have a clear goal for entering an armed conflict.
- Teachers can ask students how the Federal Reserve employs its knowledge of inflationary pressures in deciding whether to raise interest rates.
- Teachers can encourage students to apply the principle of the First Amendment of the U.S. Constitution to what the U.S. government should do if protesters organize a peaceful protest march against the government on the sidewalk of a city street.

Foreign Language

- Teachers can encourage students to use their knowledge of Japanese social customs to describe how they would introduce a friend's Japanese parents to their parents.
- Teachers can ask students how they can employ their knowledge of Latin to help build their English vocabulary.
- Teachers can tell students to use their knowledge of another language to have a conversation with a classmate about the dangers of global warming.

Art

- Teachers can ask students how advertisers use art to sell products that people don't need.
- Teachers can ask students how political cartoonists employ distortions to create humor.
- Teachers can encourage students to use their knowledge of architecture to explain the visual illusions in the construction of the Parthenon.

Music

- Teachers can ask students why supermarket executives sometimes pump music into supermarkets for people to listen to while they shop.
- Teachers can ask students how cellists employ vibrato to create a mood when they play music.

- Teachers can encourage students to apply their knowledge of timbre to describe why a clarinet sounds different from a trumpet.

Physical Education

- Teachers can ask students how they can use what they have learned about sportsmanship on the playing field in their everyday life.
- Teachers can ask students how pitchers employ psychology when they pitch balls to batters.
- Teachers can ask students how they can apply one or two rules of a game of their choice to living their lives.

Taking It to Heart

Teachers should give five examples of how to use these practical prompts in teaching.

PART III

Developing Successful Intelligence Units

The final chapters of this book may be the most important, because they lead to the actual implementation of lessons and skill building in the classroom. In these final chapters, we present the nuts and bolts of the triarchic model to assist teachers in designing and using units that facilitate the use of the three thinking skills in the classroom. In the final chapter, we include a detailed unit to demonstrate how analytical, creative, and practical intelligence skills and activities can be incorporated into classroom content. We hope that this model will stimulate your own thinking as you continue to create challenging learning experiences in your classrooms.

Framing Triarchic Instruction and Assessment Units

U p to this point, the central points of discussion of this book have been the value of the three intellectual abilities—analytical, creative, and practical—and the importance of teaching in ways that address these three abilities. If teachers agree with the idea of teaching for successful intelligence—that it is important to teach and assess triarchically—the next step is to figure out how it can be done. In this chapter, the focus changes from how to promote individual successful intelligence thinking abilities to how to design and implement lessons (or larger educational units) that develop and use these abilities in learning and thinking. A program called Triarchic Instruction and Assessment (TIA) is introduced as an implementation plan. An explanation of what TIA does and does not mean, an introduction to the steps of TIA, and extensive examples of TIA instructional and assessment materials provide teachers with a guide for developing units of instruction that promote student learning in all three abilities. (For more on TIA, see Stemler, Elliott, Grigorenko, & Sternberg, 2006; Sternberg, 2002, 2003, 2006; Sternberg & Grigorenko, 2002; Sternberg & Williams, 2001.)

THE NUTS AND BOLTS OF TIA

One approach to implementing a program of teaching successful intelligence is TIA. TIA, in addition to its specific objective of developing analytical, creative, and practical abilities, has the larger goal of preparing all learners for future success in adult life. TIA reaches a large group of learners by giving everyone a chance and by stressing the importance of both diversity and uniqueness. One of the purposes of TIA is to create a learning environment in which students can safely say, "I need to learn it another way" (instead of, "I'm never going to get it"). In turn, teachers safely can respond, "I will teach it another way" (instead of, "I'm never going to be able to teach it to him or her").

WHAT TIA MEANS

What does TIA actually mean? TIA means that the teacher finds materials that are most suitable for the development of specific abilities (analytical, creative, practical), calls on a range of abilities broader than that tapped by current educational approaches, helps student both correct and compensate for weaknesses while capitalizing on their strengths, and enhances students' motivation for learning. Make expectations clear. For example, just asking students to be, say, creative, increases their creativity, because they come to understand that they will be rewarded rather than ignored or punished when they have original ideas (O'Hara & Sternberg, 2000–2001).

Triarchic Instruction and Assessment: What It Is

- Finding suitable materials
- Calling on a range of abilities
- Helping students capitalize on their strengths
- Helping students correct or compensate for their weaknesses
- Enhancing student motivation to learn

Finding Suitable Materials

First, TIA means finding materials that are most suitable for the development of specific abilities (analytical, creative, and practical). Consider the following example.

Ms. Brown is a high school science teacher. When she teaches the structure of the atom, Ms. Brown wants to help her students capitalize on all of their abilities. She may try to develop students' analytical abilities by giving them opportunities to compare and contrast the characteristics of an electron, a proton, and a neutron. She may try to develop their creative abilities by having them imagine that an electron, a proton, and a neutron are three friends and then asking the students to describe the relationships between them. And she may try to develop their practical abilities by asking why the structure of the atom matters in the production of atomic power through nuclear fission.

Calling on a Range of Abilities

TIA means realizing the potential of people's broad ranges of abilities. The core assumption of TIA is that educators should value the diversity in students' patterns of ability. This assumption is demonstrated in the following example.

Allison was a fifth-grade student who had significant difficulty with spelling. She tried and tried to memorize the spellings of the words, but she just couldn't remember what the words looked like when she was asked to write them down. Allison rarely got a passing grade (60 percent) on her spelling tests. Then her teacher began to use TIA in her reading classes and introduced a new way of teaching spelling. Using this method, the students were to close their eyes and imagine the word. They were to associate different colors with different syllables, and they were to link different images to the word. Next, they recited the word together, syllable by syllable; only then were they asked to write the word. The imagination-based technique worked for Allison! She would close her eyes and think of a word, transforming different syllables into different colors and thinking of the various images each color pattern brought to mind. Using her imagination really paid off. Allison earned over 60 percent on all of the spelling tests linked to TIA units!

Capitalizing on Strengths and Compensating for Weaknesses

TIA also helps students capitalize on strengths and correct or compensate for weaknesses. This goal is accomplished by teaching all students in all three ways. However, TIA is not about teaching in a way that exclusively matches instruction to students' patterns of abilities. In other words, TIA does not assume that Alice should be taught only analytically, that Barbara should be taught only creatively, or that Celia should be taught only practically (from the examples in Chapter 3). TIA assumes that all three students receive triarchic instruction, which allows them to capitalize on their strengths during matching activities (analytical for Alice, creative for Barbara, and practical for Celia) and to correct or compensate for their weaknesses during "stretching" activities. For example, creative and practical assignments might initially be a challenge for Alice, but eventually she may become more comfortable doing them. And, as uncomfortable as she might be doing them, it is critical that she develop these weaker skills to the highest level that she can. She will need them to be successful.

Enhancing Motivation

TIA is intended to enhance students' motivation for learning. Teacher and student feedback on the TIA-based materials has, time and time again, shown high appreciation for the creative lessons, which allow both teacher and student to demonstrate their knowledge and their individuality. For example, one student-participant in the Expert Learning for All Through Teacher Education (ELATE) program, a literacy program based on the theory of successful intelligence and administered in Connecticut, wrote the following in her evaluation of the program after its completion:

> I felt that the creative activities allowed me to be myself. I loved coming up with ideas that allowed me to show what *I* am like and what *I* could do rather than just doing what the book wanted me to do.

WHAT TIA DOES NOT MEAN

It is important to be very clear on what TIA does *not* mean. TIA does not mean to teach the same thing three separate times, to force material to fit into a certain channel (analytical, creative, or practical), to sacrifice the acquisition and mastery of knowledge for the sake of developing thinking skills, or to equalize all students' outcomes.

Triarchic Instruction and Assessment: What It Is Not

- Teaching one thing three ways
- Forcing material to fit a particular delivery channel
- Sacrificing knowledge for thinking skills
- Equalizing outcomes for all students

Teaching Approach

It is important to understand that TIA does not mean always teaching the same word, unit, concept, or lesson three different ways. Instead, what it means is that any topic from any subject can be taught in more than one way. In reality, the reasoning behind TIA is as follows: any material (whether it deals with the understanding of decimals, the locations of countries, the functions of human organs, or the meanings of foreign words) can be taught triarchically, but certain materials are better suited for a given channel than for others. For example, a middle school math teacher teaching about large numbers might ask students to imagine that Million, Billion, Trillion, Quadrillion, and Quintillion are the characters of a new TV show. The teacher might then ask students to list two or three adjectives describing what each of the characters looks like and then describe how they are related to one another. This is a creative approach to teaching large numbers. However, because it is fairly difficult to find examples of such large numbers in everyday life, the teacher might not want to include a practical activity in teaching this lesson.

Channel Preference

Another common misconception about TIA is that all materials need to fit a certain channel (analytical, creative, or practical). TIA does not mean that material must be forced into a given channel. What is important is that throughout the day, week, and year, all three channels are used to reach every student's ability pattern. In other words, teachers stimulate learning in a preferred way and make the overall content more accessible.

Balancing Content and Skill Learning

TIA does not assume that the acquisition and mastery of content knowledge must be sacrificed for the sake of developing thinking skills. Analytical, creative, and practical thinking strategies are to be taught through the content—not instead of the content.

Outcomes

TIA stresses maximizing—not equalizing—all students' outcomes. TIA neither assumes equal achievement of students nor aims at eliminating individual differences. TIA is a tool devised to ensure content presentation in a number of ways—ways that engage students' diverse abilities. TIA allows individual learners not only to develop their strengths (by matching their individual abilities) but also to correct their weaknesses (by stretching their abilities).

THE STRUCTURE OF TIA UNITS

Introducing TIA in a classroom is about creating a supportive learning community in which students find their own ability patterns, understand how uniqueness allows each individual to make a particular contribution to the community, and learn to value diversity. As in any long-term endeavor, creating a supportive learning community is a challenging process, and TIA is only one tool among many—but it is an important one. TIA's step-by-step structure is shown in detailed discussion of its three steps: (1) pre-TIA activities, (2) designing a TIA unit, and (3) implementing TIA.

PRE-TIA ACTIVITIES

The main objective of pre-TIA activities is to initiate the formation of a specific learning niche for students. The learning niche is the most elementary unit that forms an indivisible contextual structure for students' learning. The learning niche is determined by the dominant method of instruction and assessment, the physical settings in which teaching takes place, and students' individual ability patterns. Thus, the initiation of the TIA-related learning niche includes (a) setting the stage for TIA, (b) screening the learning community for students' preferred patterns of abilities, (c) modifying the physical environment of the classroom so that it contributes to the success of TIA, and (d) preparing for the sustained effort of carrying out TIA.

Pre-TIA Activities

- Setting the stage
- Screening for students' preferred ability patterns
- Modifying the physical classroom setting
- Preparing for sustained effort

Setting the Stage for TIA

Before classes even begin, it is important that teachers set the stage with their students for a triarchically challenging classroom. They can do this by generating student interest in being different. Teachers can convince students that their teacher expects them to differ—that different patterns of abilities are accepted and success is rewarded regardless of the particular form it takes (analytical, creative, or practical). Teachers can explain that there are multiple roads to success, but that in their classrooms the criterion for success is high—students need to master the content somehow (analytically, creatively, or practically).

Teachers can encourage students to succeed within TIA by consistently offering chances to develop all three abilities (analytical, creative, or practical) and by testing their achievement in all three ways. It is both teachers' and students' shared responsibility to invest effort in learning via each of the three channels.

Characteristics of the TIA Learning Community

The TIA learning community is a community in which students:

- Have a chance to show who they are and, therefore, have enhanced confidence
- Feel accepted
- Accept, understand, and value other members of the community
- Persist in the face of failure and look for alternative ways to master difficult materials
- Redefine difficult learning situations to maximize success
- Know and balance their personal strengths and weaknesses
- Work hard on developing their strengths and compensating for their weaknesses

---

Screening Students for Ability Profiles

TIA is not just about matching. TIA is about teaching in multiple ways so that students experience learning in both preferred and nonpreferred ways. Yet it helps teachers and students to know the students' patterns of abilities, that is, their strengths and weaknesses. An awareness of students' self-reported strengths and weaknesses can help teachers better understand, monitor, and encourage individual pathways of learning. Students may find that an awareness of their patterns of abilities helps them structure their learning activities better and get more satisfaction from school.

There are many traditional ways teachers can elicit this information from students and encourage awareness. Among these traditional techniques are reflection time, journal writing, discussions, and lesson evaluations. The main objective of these activities is to accustom students to sharing their learning preferences, their strengths and weaknesses, and their likes and dislikes. The following two strategies may be useful in discovering student ability patterns.

Strategy 1: Teachers can ask students to indicate activities they like to do (see box on p. 144 for examples of activities by ability). It is preferred that teachers not identify the ability the question indicates and not mix the questions from the different abilities on the question sheet given to the students. The activities appeal to a wide range of ages, from grade schoolers to high schoolers. Teachers should create their own lists based on the age and educational level of their students.

Sample Activity List for Eliciting Student Learning Preferences: Strategy 1

Things I Like to Do

Please read the list and mark the activities you like to do. Do not mark activities you do not like to do.

I like . . .

Analytical

- Analyzing characters when I'm reading or listening to a story
- Comparing and contrasting points of view
- Criticizing my own and other kids' work
- Thinking clearly and analytically
- Appealing to logic
- Evaluating my and others' points of view
- Judging my and other kids' behavior
- Explaining difficult problems to other kids
- Solving logical problems
- Making inferences and deriving conclusions
- Sorting and classifying
- Thinking about things

Creative

- Designing new things
- Coming up with ideas
- Using my imagination
- Playing make-believe and pretend games
- Thinking of alternative solutions
- Noticing things people usually tend to ignore
- Thinking in pictures and images
- Inventing (new recipes, words, games)
- Supposing that things were different
- Thinking about what would have happened if certain aspects of the world were different
- Composing (new songs, melodies)
- Acting and role-playing

Practical

- Taking things apart and fixing them
- Learning through hands-on activities
- Making and maintaining friends
- Understanding and respecting others
- Putting into practice things I have learned
- Resolving conflicts
- Advising my friends on their problems
- Convincing someone to do something
- Learning by interacting with others
- Applying my knowledge
- Working and being with others
- Adapting to new situations

Strategy 2: Teachers can ask students to respond to a hypothetical situation in which a number of roles must be filled. Students are to indicate whom they would choose for each role from among their classmates and the reason they made a particular choice (see box below for an example situation).

Sample Activity Sheet for Eliciting Student Learning Preferences: Strategy 2

Form a Team

Suppose you are on a mission to Mars. You will be in space for a long period of time, you have serious tasks to accomplish, and you need to come back on time. You are the captain and you need to form a team of three members (selected from your classmates), including you. The skills that must be present in the crew are (a) analyzing situations and thinking clearly and logically, (b) inventing and designing new things in unexpected situations, and (c) fixing things when they break (or knowing how to get along with other people).

Which skill requirement do you think you qualify for (circle one)?
(a) (b) (c)

Which of your classmates would you select as team member 1?
Which skill requirement do you think he or she qualifies for (circle one)?
(a) (b) (c)

Which of your classmates would you select as team member 2?
Which skill requirement do you think he or she qualifies for (circle one)?
(a) (b) (c)

Modifying the Physical Setting of the Classroom

If teachers have the luxury of teaching in their own classroom, they may consider modifying its physical setting to help students remember that it is a place where different kinds of abilities all matter. For example, teachers can post stories about untraditional thinkers, clips about practical applications of the content being taught, or open-ended questions such as "What if . . . ?" Teachers can do whatever they think might help their students understand that diversity in abilities is welcome in the classroom.

Preparing to Make a Sustained Effort to Implement TIA

TIA may seem a bit of a departure from regular lesson planning routines, and the lessons may look, sound, and feel somewhat different. Many teachers who have participated in TIA programs have observed that, even though TIA has stretched their curricula, made them aware of their own preferences in teaching, and showed them ways to enhance various kinds of learning, it has also required ongoing effort. Teachers have also observed that at times it is a challenge to sustain this effort. This challenge stems in part from the need for self-discipline to ensure the presence of analytical, creative, and practical components in what is taught and assessed. Teachers have also encountered occasional resistance from students reluctant to deviate from learning routines acquired over years of learning in conventional ways.

On the other hand, many teachers have also discovered that the more they have created TIA lessons, the more natural and easy it has become to design the units. Over time, the TIA stockpile in their bag of teaching tricks has grown. Their teaching has become richer, they have stretched and enhanced their teaching repertoire, and, consequently, they have modified the learning process in their classrooms so that learning has become more engaging, more fun, and more productive for their students. See the box below for some informal feedback from teachers and students who have participated in TIA programs (Grigorenko, Jarvin, & Sternberg, 2002).

Teacher and Student Feedback on TIA Programs

Teachers' Responses

Teachers scored the following questions on a scale of 1 (strongly disagree) through 7 (strongly agree). The averages of their responses are included following each question.

Did you find TIA . . .

interesting to you?	6.41
interesting to your students?	5.99
motivating to you?	6.19
motivating to your students?	6.12
suggestive of alternative teaching strategies addressing the needs of students with various levels of skills?	5.88
inclusive of a wide range of students?	5.85

Teachers' Comments

"I like TIA activities because they are well organized, provide constant reinforcement of skills, encourage higher-level thinking, and develop creativity" (KC, middle school teacher).

"I like TIA activities because they focus on different learners, allow students to build on their strengths, and provide wonderful group activities (which can also be done individually)" (AC, middle school teacher).

Students' Responses

Students completed the following questionnaire, and the percentage of students who circled each item is indicated following that item.

How did you like the activities introduced by TIA? (Circle one.)

I liked the activities very much.	35.0%
I liked the activities.	50.8%
I did not care one way or another.	10.0%
I disliked the activities.	1.7%
I hated the activities.	2.5%

DESIGNING A TIA UNIT

How exactly does a teacher develop a triarchic unit? Is it any different from developing any unit or any lesson? The answer is both no and yes. No, because as in planning any lesson, designing a triarchic lesson consists of traditional routines such as determining the content, objectives, and time line of the unit. Yes, because in addition to going through traditional steps of lesson planning, teachers need to get accustomed to teaching and assessing for analytical, creative, and practical abilities. The steps of planning a triarchic unit are summarized in the box below. Although these steps are just suggestions (as is the case with any recipe, the maker can deviate from them), they represent the best experiences in planning TIA units from some of those who have done it.

Recipe for a TIA Unit

Ingredients: content, objectives, time

Directions:

1. Determine the content to be taught. What is the content that I need to teach in this unit?

2. Define objectives. What do students have to learn (both knowledge and skills)? What do I want students to learn? What do students want to learn?

3. Specify a time line. Within what time frame do I want these objectives to be accomplished?

4. Divide the unit into lessons and structure the lessons by type: explanation/discovery, practice, students' self-study, assessment. How many lessons can I spend on this unit? How do I want to structure this unit? Will the unit include lectures? Will the unit include group activities? Will the unit include homework? What kinds of assessment will the unit include?

5. Determine which learning channels are most suitable for which components of the content. Generate a list of triarchic (analytical, creative, and practical) activities that span the content of the unit.

6. Decide how to incorporate the learning channels into the transmission of the material. Sequence triarchic activities. Consider logical sequence, lesson flow, and the dynamics of learning. Balance the unit using a variety of lesson elements.

7. Design matching assessments. Use various types of assessments to measure student learning.

Determine the Content to Be Taught

Using the guidelines of the state, district, or school, teachers should define the content to be taught in a given triarchic unit. For example, a

high school art teacher may be asked to design a unit on impressionism; a high school history teacher, a unit on the Persian Gulf War.
After dividing the broad topic into its components, teachers have the
big picture as well as the details to assist in planning each individual
lesson.

Define Objectives

Teachers need to ask themselves, "What (knowledge and skills) do
I want my students to master in this unit?" Teachers may have very broad
objectives (e.g., "I want my students to familiarize themselves with the
school of impressionism" or "I want to teach my students how to solve
problems using primary historical sources") or relatively narrow objectives (e.g., "I want my students to know that there is another, human side
to the war in Iraq—that soldiers who fight there leave behind their normal
lives and those who come home are changed forever by their war experiences"; or "I want my students to know how to make lists"; or "I want my
students to know how to read charts").

Teachers might have their students generate unit objectives. See the
box below for a technique to elicit learning objectives from students. For
example, if the plan is to teach a unit on statistics, teachers might ask
their students what they would like to know about statistics and how they
might like to apply statistical knowledge. Allowing students to direct their
own learning gives them a sense of involvement in teaching and a sense
of ownership in their learning. When the unit is complete, teachers can
provide students with an opportunity to reflect on the unit and their
learning processes by instructing them to write about what they have
learned.

Student Worksheet for Eliciting Learning Objectives and Reflecting on What Has Been Learned

Topic: Name: Date:

Knew before: What I already know about the topic

What I want to know: What I wonder/would like to know about the topic

Know now: What I have learned about the topic

Specify the Time Line

As in any lesson planning, in TIA planning it is important that teachers specify the time line for the unit. They can do this by considering how much time can be spent on or is reasonable to spend on the unit. If the unit is a one-lesson unit, perhaps some triarchic activities can be blended together. For example, if a teacher is designing a home economics unit, she can combine creative and practical activities in a group activity focused on planning a family celebration. If the unit is fairly long, specific lessons can be dedicated to certain types of activities. For example, if a teacher is creating a language arts lesson about a work of fiction, he can design an analytical lesson analyzing the book's characters and settings, a practical lesson linking the characters' and the students' experiences, and a creative lesson requiring students to extend the story beyond what the author has written.

Divide the Unit Into Lessons and Structure the Lessons by Type

After determining the time line of the unit, teachers need to ask how many lessons can be devoted to the unit and how to structure those lessons by type—that is, explanation/discovery, practice, students' self-study, and assessment. As the unit is divided into lessons, teachers should choose how many explanation/exploration and practice/training lessons to give and decide how to assess students' progress. For example, a middle school teacher using one of the basal textbooks to teach reading might distribute time among lessons as follows: one lesson introduces the story, provides necessary background information, and explains vocabulary; two lessons provide vocabulary practice and comprehension enhancement (through spelling and creative writing); and one lesson assesses vocabulary and comprehension. Teachers might want to determine which lessons will include lectures, which will include group activities, and which will involve individual work.

Determine Suitable Learning Channels

After the unit's objectives, time line, and lesson structure are defined, the next step is for teachers to create analytical, creative, and practical activities and assessment items. (See the box below for a guide for planning items by type.) For example, when teaching about impressionism, an art teacher may want to include analytical activities that involve comparing and contrasting Chevreul's theory of the chromatic circle and Delacroix's theory of primary and secondary colors, creative activities that require students to design new shades of color from primary colors, and practical problem-solving activities involving colors, such as how to dye a T-shirt or how to paint a room. As each activity is devised, teachers should be sure to specify its objective to students. It is also important for teachers to remember that it is not essential to teach every lesson in all three ways. Instead, teachers should create activities that best fit the lesson content and learning objectives. If a creative activity does not fit the content, teachers should not force it. For example, a modern history teacher may decide to teach a lesson on genocide without a creative component. If there is just not enough time for, say, an analytical activity, teachers can simply skip it. But then they should not forget to include an analytical lesson in the next unit.

Planning Form for Generating Analytical, Creative, and Practical Activities

Unit: Date:

Content/objectives:

Activities mapped to objectives:

Analytical

Objective:

Activity:

Objective:

Activity:

Creative

Objective:

Activity:

Objective:

Activity:

Practical

Objective:

Activity:

Objective:

Activity:

Some examples of both in-class and homework instructional materials are provided in the boxes below. These materials help students develop analytical, creative, and practical thinking skills that they can apply directly to their reading. These examples are based on a story from the textbook *Light Up the Sky* (Farr & Strickland, 1993). Although activities are classified loosely as analytical, creative, and practical, these classifications represent emphases rather than fully discrete categories. Ultimately, students need to combine these skills rather than use them separately.

Examples of In-Class Instructional Materials

These materials are used in class to develop analytical, creative, and practical thinking skills to apply to reading.

Analytical

Analytical exercises develop analysis, judgment, and comparison skills. The following exercise helps students learn to develop these skills in collaboration with other students.

> Divide the students into small groups and give each group a big piece of poster board and assorted colored pens and pencils. Tell the students that they are to spend time with their groups making a "portrait" of their assigned character. Emphasize that they should use their own understanding of the character based on the details in the story itself. Stress that they should focus on what the words in the story tell them about the character. Tell the students that when they present their character, they will also be expected to retell the events their character experienced in the story.

(For this and many other examples from the literacy programs based on the theory of successful intelligence, go to http://pace.tufts.edu, click on "Materials" under the heading "Resources," and when the Materials page opens, click on "Summerbridge Project" for rising sixth-graders or "Light Up the Sky" for fifth-graders.)

Creative

The goal in the creative items is not for students to generate "correct" answers, but for them to fantasize about and invent imaginative answers. In this exercise, students are asked to provide their own "words of wisdom" on challenging problems to which they are unlikely to know the correct answers.

Words of Wisdom

By (write your name here) _____

Why are there rainbows after a storm? How do rainbows get to be so many different colors? How can you get the pot of gold at the end of a rainbow?

Why do cows say *moo* all the time? Why does this one word play such a big part in cow language? What are the cows saying?

Practical

The goal here is to encourage students to think of the practical facets of what they read. The following exercise helps develop route planning skills.

Remind the students that, as they have learned, many slaves ran away from their masters and fled to the North, often with the assistance of the Underground Railroad. Tell the students that they are going to do a small-group exercise to think more about what it actually must have been like to run away from slavery. Each group is to imagine that they are to plan for a slave to travel from slavery in North Carolina to freedom in Canada using a map, a set of tools, and a set of survival rules.

Examples of Homework Instructional Materials

These homework materials help students develop analytical, creative, and practical thinking skills on their own.

Analytical

In the following exercise, students reflect on an experience and then describe, analyze, and communicate it so that another individual can understand it.

Tell students: Suppose you have just spent a special holiday with your relatives and friends. Your favorite cousin could not be there because he is in the army and is stationed far away. Write your

(Continued)

(Continued)

cousin a letter fully describing and analyzing the big day so that he will feel as if he had been there.

Creative

The students have read a story about the Bell family that refers to some good times and bad times. But these events are not fully described. The students are asked to expand the story and invent descriptions of these events.

Tell students: The story is, in part, about the Bells' family history— the good times and bad times they have experienced living along the National Road for generations. Think of at least one good time and one bad time referred to in the story. As fully as you can, describe what these events may have been like and explain their importance to the Bell family.

Practical

An important part of everyday life is preparing for major events. In the story the students have read, the Bells are preparing for a major celebration. Students are asked to place themselves in the role of the Bells and describe what they would do to prepare for a big family gathering.

Tell students: In the story, the Bells have a large family gathering, full of food and different activities. It takes a lot of planning to put on such a big event. Pretend you are Jason's parents and you are hosting the event. Describe some things you would do to prepare.

Incorporate Learning Channels Into the Transmission of Material

Yet another step in devising a triarchic unit is to sequence the activities. Teachers need to ask: Which activity comes first? Which activity will effectively introduce the topic of the unit, set up the unit's context, and motivate students? What is the best way to close the unit? Which activity would create a good link to the next unit? Do students need direct instruction before they can engage in a creative activity, or will a creative activity help them explore the topic and better prepare them for direct instruction?

As activities are ordered, teachers need to keep the following four-pronged model of effective instruction in mind:

1. Tell me. Teachers explain to students what the unit's objectives are and what they are to know or to master by the end of the unit. (For example, "I want you to know how to create lists in your writing.")

2. Show me. Teachers show students what the targeted skills are. (For example, "Let's do a list together. Let's compile a list of our favorite foods.")

3. Guide me. Teachers supervise students' practice. (For example, "Now make a list of your favorite activities. Remember that the requirements for the list include . . .")

4. Challenge me. Teachers test students' knowledge. (For example, "Now each of you needs to think of a list you want to make and show me your list.")

Teachers should remember that nothing is quite done even when it is done! There is no doubt that even as the lesson is delivered, new things and new information will be discovered—so teachers should be prepared to modify as they go along. Even the best TIA plans sometimes go amiss.

Design Matching Assessments

Teachers should remember that the ultimate goal of TIA is to contribute to the development of a triarchic thinker. Therefore, when teachers create assessments, they need to focus on how to evaluate students' products to ensure the development of their thinking through all three channels—analytical, creative, and practical.

What is a good answer? Teachers can begin by setting up prototypes for a good answer, a basic answer, and a deficient answer (see box below). Teachers can then share these categories with their students.

Assessing a Triarchic Thinker's Response

A good answer:

- Demonstrates the student's thorough understanding of the material
- Uses analytical thinking to make logical assumptions and draw conclusions, make inferences, and compare the ideas of the students with those of other people

---

(Continued)

(Continued)

- Connects new material to personal experiences for practical applications of knowledge
- Goes beyond the known

A basic answer:

- Demonstrates an understanding of the basic points of the material
- Demonstrates a firm understanding of the new material but has no links or weak links to previously acquired knowledge
- Shows a plausible grasp of the content and the details of the new material but does not show inferences
- Does not connect the new material to personal experiences
- Does not extend the material creatively

A deficient answer:

- Demonstrates confusion and a lack of understanding of the material
- Contains bits of unrelated information
- Does not isolate the main idea
- Does not refer to relevant details
- Does not analyze ideas
- Does not use practical applications
- Is not creative

Three different answers for three types of questions are analyzed below to show how this classification works in practice. The example assessments were developed as part of a TIA program to teach Irene Hunt's novel *The Lottery Rose* (1992). (A summary of the plot is provided below to help you understand the examples.)

Summary of *The Lottery Rose* by Irene Hunt

Georgie Burgess is severely abused by his mother and her boyfriend, Steve. Even Georgie's teacher, Miss Cressman, thinks he is stupid and treats him accordingly. Georgie copes by withdrawing into a safe and secret world of beautiful gardens filled with roses, just like those in the library books he treasures.

One day, Georgie wins a small rosebush in a lottery held at the grocery store where the kind Mrs. Sims works. After a particularly brutal beating from Steve, Georgie goes to live with Mr. and Mrs. Sims, a childless family in the neighborhood who takes a liking to him. But, because the couple cannot afford to adopt a child, Georgie goes to a home for boys run by Sister Mary Angela.

In her wisdom, Sister Mary Angela assigns her "public relations boy," Timothy, to be Georgie's guide around school. The two become close friends. While at the new school, Georgie finds the perfect place to plant his "lottery rose"—across the street from the school in Mrs. Harper's garden. Mr. Collier, Mrs. Harper's father, explains that his daughter may not like the new rosebush because the garden became her sacred sanctuary after a car accident killed her husband and young son. Sure enough, when Mrs. Harper sees Georgie's rosebush in her private garden, she is angered and uproots the precious bush from the garden, thus losing Georgie's trust.

Through his close relationships with Sister Mary Angela, Timothy, and Mr. Collier, Georgie learns to trust people and to believe in himself. Eventually, he forgives Mrs. Harper for her initial anger, and their relationship provides each of them with much-needed love and mutual understanding.

The first example assesses analytical thinking.

An Analytical Thinking Assessment Example

Question

Why do you think Sister Mary Angela chooses Timothy to be Georgie's guide around the school?

Children's Sample Answers

1. I think Timothy is a friendly, understanding boy whose attitude toward people is very different from the other boys'. He's quiet and meek but can give a lot of sympathy to people who need it.

2. Because Timothy is Georgie's friend.

3. Because Sister Mary Angela knew that they would get along good.

Using the answer guidelines shown above, the first answer is interpreted as a good answer because the student shows fine understanding of the material, draws conclusions, and makes inferences. The novel does not provide explicit descriptions of Timothy's character but portrays the boy's interactions with other people. This student's extraction of knowledge about Timothy's character demonstrates strong analytical thinking. The second answer is viewed as a deficient answer. At the time of Georgie's tour around the school, Timothy and Georgie had not yet become friends. Thus, this answer demonstrates confusion and a lack of understanding of the material. The third answer is viewed as a basic answer. This student grasped the idea that Sister Mary Angela is a good judge of character but did not support this conclusion with any analysis.

The second example assesses creative thinking.

A Creative Thinking Assessment Example

Question

Suppose Mr. Collier is writing a note to Miss Cressman to give her an update on her former student, Georgie. What might the note say?

Children's Sample Answers

1. If Mr. Collier were to write Miss Cressman, I think he would tell her that Georgie had shown a lot of improvement in school and in relating to people, and he wouldn't let on that Georgie still really doesn't like her. He might include Georgie's literary level, along with his written progress and a list of the books he's read.

2. Georgie is doing great. He learned how to read and he is making more progress every day.

3. He doesn't participate in his classes.

The first answer is an example of a good answer. The student reflects on Georgie's current achievements but suggests keeping the peace with Georgie's former teacher by not bringing up how hurt and angry Georgie still feels about his experiences in Miss Cressman's class. The student makes inferences beyond what is stated in the book. The second answer is a basic answer; it demonstrates only minimal understanding of the material. The third answer is an example of a deficient answer. This student reflects on selected superficial facts of the novel and does not mention Georgie's overall academic progress.

The third example assesses practical abilities.

A Practical Assessment Example

Question

What advice would you give Georgie about adjusting to his new home at the boys' school?

Children's Sample Answers

1. You should be patient with the other boys and try to bond with people. If you make friends, the change will be easier and may be fun; after all, this home is a lot better than the one you lived in before. Most important, try to be optimistic about every good thing about this home, and try to be sociable.

2. Try to make friends and love one another and you will get love in return.

3. Try to trust people more and don't be afraid.

The first answer is a good answer because the student demonstrates thorough understanding of the material by addressing Georgie's weakest qualities (pessimism, withdrawal, and resistance to forming friendships). Both the second and third answers are basic answers, because they demonstrate basic understanding of the material but fail to address the specific characteristics that hinder Georgie's adjustment to the new school.

Triarchic Assessment

As noted, one crucial component of TIA is triarchic assessment. Assessments can take a variety of forms (e.g., quizzes, tests, compositions, performances, portfolios, process folios), but every TIA assessment should follow one rule without exception: *mastery of both basic content and understanding using all three abilities must be assessed.* In order to maintain students' motivation for learning, teachers should evaluate them for *how* as well as *what* material is learned!

Any triarchic assessment should include assessment via memory-based items. This is important because (a) the ultimate goal of education is the mastery of knowledge, and memory will always play a crucial role in learning—therefore, testing for memory is very important; (b) the overwhelming majority of district and statewide school tests and virtually all standardized tests encountered in school and elsewhere contain memory-based items—therefore, teachers need to prepare their students for this type of testing; and (c) the best way to show that TIA enhances memorization and mastery of content more effectively than does traditional teaching is to include memory-based items in assessments following triarchic units.

Examples of Memory Items

1. The following time line lists events in the story in the order in which they happened.
   - Georgie gets a lottery ticket at the grocery store.
   - Georgie wins a rosebush.
   - Steve brutally beats Georgie.
   - _____
   - Georgie goes to live at the home for boys run by Sister Mary Angela.

   Which of the following events belongs in the blank above?
      a. Georgie sets a fire under Miss Cressman's car.
      b. Georgie lives temporarily with Mr. and Mrs. Sims.
      c. Georgie tries to plant his bush in Mrs. Harper's garden.
      d. Georgie goes to the store to buy pork and beans.

2. Mrs. Harper performs a number of caring deeds to help Georgie and perhaps win his forgiveness and trust. Which of the following is NOT one of Mrs. Harper's deeds?
      a. Mrs. Harper helps Sister Mary Angela care for Georgie during his fever.
      b. Mrs. Harper allows Georgie's rosebush to be planted in her garden.
      c. Mrs. Harper sings for Georgie.
      d. Mrs. Harper pays Georgie's school expenses for a year.

Experienced TIA implementers have no difficulty designing analytical, creative, and practical units. Although designing triarchic items is challenging at first, it becomes increasingly automatic. The authors have not yet come across a topic that cannot be taught and assessed triarchically. Teachers should remember these general principles:

1. Don't be afraid of overlap. Because different components of triarchic instruction address the same broad content, analytical,

creative, and practical lessons (including assignments and assessments) will inevitably overlap.

2. Don't target one ability exclusively (i.e., don't try to come up with "pure" analytical, creative, or practical lessons). Try to provide scaffolding for all three abilities while primarily stressing one ability or perhaps two abilities at most (i.e., come up with lessons that prioritize specific abilities).

3. Match assessments with teaching, making sure that achievement is assessed through all three channels; call on all three abilities and weigh them about equally.

4. Use a variety of assessment methods (e.g., essay, short-answer exams, projects, performances, portfolios).

IMPLEMENTING TIA

The most enjoyable part of TIA is delivering triarchic lessons and watching students show abilities they have not evidenced before. Following are a few tips for teachers on how to make the presentation of TIA most effective:

1. While teaching, blend analytical, creative, and practical abilities in equal (or almost equal) amounts in everything done in the classroom.

2. While assessing students, have equally high but realistic standards for students' analytical, creative, and practical work.

3. If students have difficulty accepting the TIA, show patience (e.g., don't answer your own questions; don't perform activities for the students).

4. Persevere (e.g., don't give up because the going initially gets tough).

5. Support students' efforts (e.g., acknowledge effort and signs of progress).

Another very important part of TIA is reflection. Teachers should take the time to reflect on the TIA unit and make note of everything that worked and did not work. Teachers should do this after each TIA unit. Teachers can consider engaging students in this activity, but they should be careful not to burden students with endless evaluations and reflections. Using a reflection form may help teachers reflect on the strengths and weaknesses of the unit. The trick is for teachers to take brief notes as a TIA unit is presented, and then to summarize students' impressions and comments. This task should not be put off until the unit is over! If this happens, enriching details will slip away.

Sample Reflection Forms for Teachers

Reflection Form 1

Unit: _____ Date(s):_____

- Things that worked
- Things that did not work
- Things to be changed

Example of a Completed Teacher Action Log

- The teacher action log helps you (a) reflect on the status of your objectives, (b) summarize where you are and where you need to go, and (c) determine your next set of objectives.

M = memory, A = analytical, C = creative, P = practical

Objective	Activity	Date	Level of Mastery (Satisfaction)	Label
to teach long-vowel sounds in spelling	SL1	2/3	75%	M
vocabulary	VL1	2/5	80%	M/A/P/C
dealing with dilemmas	GA	5/8	(90% part) worked	A/P
words of wisdom	GA	5/10	need to reflect/ resolve	A/C

Sample Reflection Form for Students

Name: Week (Lesson):   Date:

I learned . . .

I want to learn more about . . .

I liked . . .

I did not like . . .

I did not understand . . .

I think I'd like the lesson more if . . .

Putting It All Together

*A Comprehensive Illustration
of Lessons for Teaching for
Successful Intelligence*

Now that teachers have mastered the craft of TIA, this chapter provides a one-week portion of a TIA unit developed for sixth-graders. For three weeks, these students worked with *A Raisin in the Sun*, a screenplay by Lorraine Hansberry (1994). In this example, in-class instructional materials, a homework assignment, a comprehension assessment, and the author's commentaries are provided. To find the rest of the unit, go to the Web site http://pace.tufts.edu, find the heading "Resources" in the left-hand column, and click on "Materials" underneath this heading.

INTRODUCTION TO THE UNIT

As in any new unit, this TIA unit starts with the delivery of basic background information. Following is a summary of the story used as the basis of the example in this chapter.

Summary of *A Raisin in the Sun* by Lorraine Hansberry

A Raisin in the Sun is the story of the Youngers, an African American family living in a Chicago ghetto in the 1950s. Lena Younger is the recently widowed matriarch of the family. Lena shares a crowded apartment with her two children, Walter and Beneatha, her daughter-in-law Ruth, and her grandson Travis.

When the late Mr. Younger's life insurance check arrives in the mail, a conflict arises among the family members as to how the money should be spent. Lena takes one third of the money and buys a house in Clybourne Park, a predominantly white neighborhood. She gives Walter the rest of the money to be divided equally between himself and Beneatha. Walter's dream of quitting his job as a chauffeur and starting his own business collapses when his business partner skips town with the insurance money. To make matters worse, Walter had given Beneatha's share to his "friend" as well—the money she had planned to use for her medical school tuition.

In the midst of this turmoil, Mr. Lindner arrives at the Youngers' apartment on behalf of the Clybourne Park Improvement Association. He offers to pay the family more than the house is worth in order to keep "colored folk" out of the neighborhood. This intimidation and antagonism at a time when the family is in dire financial straits threatens to crush the family, and they are tempted to sell their dream house. But at the last minute Walter takes command, and in a display of pride and understanding, tells Mr. Lindner that they refuse to sell. The Youngers are left with the house and, more important, a renewed sense of dignity.

UNIT LESSON 1: INTRODUCTION

The objective of this first lesson is to prepare students to read the book by introducing both the context and the new vocabulary of the play. Teachers can reach these objectives by following the outline below. The shaded text indicates actual unit material.

Basic Introduction to the Screenplay

- Give the students some background information about the screenplay's author, setting (Chicago in the 1950s), and subject matter (African Americans' struggles to survive and achieve their dreams in the face of discrimination and economic difficulty).

- Make sure that the students understand that, although Lorraine Hansberry originally wrote *A Raisin in the Sun* as a play, this is her screenplay version. It is written to be used as a blueprint for a director creating a motion picture. Also make sure that the students follow and understand the format:

  1. The writing in all capital letters is to direct the camera.
  2. Dialogue for the actors is indented, in the center of the page, and introduced with the speaking character's name.
  3. Directions for the actors are in italics.

- You may want to enlist the help of students who have been involved in film or stage production. If you have any such students in your class, you can get them to explain the format. To help the students grasp what a screenplay is, bring a copy of a screenplay from a film the students are likely to have seen. Large bookstores generally have copies of the screenplays of recent blockbuster films.

Begin Reading the Play

- Perhaps spend some time reading and analyzing Hansberry's opening shot—particularly the meaning and effect of the superimposed Langston Hughes poem. Get the students to predict what the story is about, in light of the poem. Ask: What/how does the poem make them feel? What is the effect of having the poem appear line by line? Why is the last line in italics? And so on.
- Explain and assign different roles for the week. For example, use these roles:

  Discussion Director (leads and orchestrates the discussion)

  Vocabulary Enricher (investigates and explains the meaning of new words)

  Illustrator (provides illustrations for scenes—either in drawings or in words)

  Summarizer (summarizes the new material for the class)

  Investigator (finds relevant information not included in the book)

  Travel Tracer (tracks the movement of the characters)

- You also may want to provide your Investigator with some of the supplementary materials or instruct him or her how to use the library or Internet to find relevant material. Each week of the program the Investigator may need some initial guidance so that he or she can perform his or her role. Of course, there are other roles you can

(Continued)

(Continued)

come up with, and some in this list could be eliminated. Have one student in the class do each role. Depending on the size of your class, you may have to add to these assignments or skip some of them. You can ask for volunteers for the different jobs, but tell the students that they can't do the same job twice. The following week they will have to select a different role.

- Instruct students to keep a reading journal and character chart.

   1. In the journal, students can write down their reactions to the play as well as any problems or questions they may have and take notes as appropriate on class discussions and activities.

   2. The students should keep and gradually add information to a character chart as they read. The characters (listed along the y-axis of the chart) are Walter, Beneatha, Lena, and Ruth. More minor characters are Travis, Mrs. Holiday, Asagai, Herman, Mrs. Johnson, George Murchison, and Karl Lindner. A short list of "items to note" about characters appears along the x-axis of the chart: (a) Who is this? (e.g., "so-and-so's brother"); (b) What is he or she like? (e.g., quiet, selfish, talkative, angry, tired); (c) phrases, sentences, or events that reveal character (e.g., things he or she says or does that show what he or she is really like); (d) character's "problem" (e.g., what does he or she want, care for; what motivates or drives this person?); and (e) points of change (e.g., moments or events that show that this person is changing in some way).

- Begin reading. There is about a page and a half of description to read before dialogue begins. Once the dialogue begins, it might be a good idea to assign a different student to read each character's part and encourage the students to read "in character."

- A list of words drawn from the first week's reading is shown here. They constitute a sampling of words that students may find challenging or unfamiliar. The number of the page where the word appears is given in parentheses. This vocabulary list is meant to be suggestive rather than definitive. Your student Vocabulary Enricher will identify some new words, but you may want to use this list to help you choose a few additional words for discussion.

deferred (3)	multiplicity (4)
fester (3)	determined (8)
syrupy (3)	listlessly (8)
accommodate (4)	indifference (12)
tenement (4)	prevail (12)

feisty (12)

counterpoint (12)

dejection (14)

ominous (15)

aloof (16)

unabashed (16)

condescending (20)

imperiously (20)

harassing (21)

draughty (30)

reflectively (34)

briskly (34)

disbelief (35)

glistening (39)

overdue (38)

gall (40)

luxurious (43)

furnishings (43)

leisurely (43)

affluence (44)

immaculate (44)

chauffeur (46)

sullenly (46)

amiably (47)

petulant (49)

disparaging (50)

haughtily (51)

bland (52)

simmering (52)

bandits (54)

envy (54)

resolutely (57)

overhead (62)

meddled (65)

placated (64)

duality (68)

decrepit (69)

raucous (72)

intimidated (77)

tyrant (77)

dreary (80)

valiant (80)

- Assign reading. The first third of the book (and a good stopping point) is at about page 80 (right where the pictures from the movie begin in the text). If you think this is an unreasonable amount of reading to assign for one night, you could break it in half somewhere; for example, you could assign pages 1 through 45 the first evening (ending just after Walter's at-work scene and before we get a glimpse of Beneatha at college) and pages 46 through 80 the following evening.

In this particular unit, analytical, creative, and practical activities are separated. As mentioned before, this separation is not necessary and is not always even desirable. In this particular program, the luxury of spending each of three lessons on activities centered around a specific ability was available—please note that the activities are not completely independent of each other, but rather each of them has a particular spin, depending on which ability is addressed. To stress this fact, the types of abilities evoked by a given activity are shown.

UNIT LESSON 2: ANALYTICAL

The objectives of the second lesson are to (a) build vocabulary, (b) enhance comprehension of the material, and (c) elicit the development of analytical skills (compare and contrast, name likes and dislikes, understand main characters, analyze the author's intentions). Teachers can reach these objectives by following the outline below.

Discuss the Reading

- Discuss and analyze the reading. Exact content will vary, depending on how far in the screenplay the students have read at this point and what their particular interests and problems with the reading were.
- Call for contributions from each student in his or her designated role (e.g., your Vocabulary Enhancer should have new words for you). (Memory/Analytical)
- Elicit personal reactions. Ask students—remind them to look in their journals if they can't remember—what their reactions to the play were: What did they like/dislike? What emotions did the play make them feel? Could they relate personally to any of the characters in the play or to any of the events that transpired? Were there parts or moments of the play that confused them or that they just couldn't follow? Discuss all of these things. (Analytical/Practical)
- Discuss the characters. Get the students to tell you by looking at their character charts what they know about the characters so far. Ask: What are the different characters like? How can you tell? What is this character's central problem in life? What drives him or her? Make a master character chart on the board or hang a chart somewhere in the room where the students can see it. (Memory/Analytical)
- Discuss societal issues. Get the students to talk about what this screenplay reveals about African American life in the middle of the twentieth century. (Use supplementary materials. This may also be a good time to call on your Investigator.) Ask: What have students learned about job opportunities for African Americans at that point in our nation's history? Are things different today or not? Consider putting a chart on the board to compare and contrast "then" and "now." (Analytical)
- Discuss problematic vocabulary. This may come up when you call on your Vocabulary Enhancer. It seems that much of the difficult vocabulary in the screenplay appears in the author's instructions to the actors (e.g., on page 17, "with a magnanimous wave of the hand"). If some words that are part of actors' instructions do come

up, you might want to consider getting a student to volunteer to act out the direction in a way that shows the meaning of the word. Students may enjoy this, and such an exercise may reinforce the meaning of these words. (Analytical/Practical)

- Initiate a discussion about the author's intentions or craft. For example, ask the students why the author included a particular scene, and see if you can get them to think about how that scene functions in the play—that is, what it specifically reveals or accomplishes. Ask them what they might have done differently. (Analytical/Creative)

UNIT LESSON 3: PRACTICAL

Discovering the practical meaning of mastered material—finding its fit in students' lives—is crucial to TIA units. For any knowledge to be internalized and appropriated by students, students need to relate it to their own lives. There are many ways of doing this: (a) ask students if anything from the reading is relevant to their lives; (b) ask students if anything in the book resembles something that has happened to people they know; or (c) ask students to pretend that they are the main characters of the screenplay and need to solve their dilemmas for themselves. The objectives of this lesson are to (a) build vocabulary, (b) enhance comprehension of the material, and (c) elicit the development of practical skills (persuade, advise, handle). Following are various activities teachers can use for practical lessons.

Practical Exercise: What to Do With the Money

Debate and Persuasion

- Stage a debate. By now, the students should grasp that one of the central dilemmas of the book is what Mrs. Younger should do with her newfound wealth. Tell the students that they're going to have a chance to exercise their powers of persuasion by participating in a debate on this subject. There are various ways a debate such as this one could be structured. One idea is to put the students in three small groups. Explain to them that each group is the representative—or agent, lawyer, spokesperson, or whichever term you think the students

(Continued)

(Continued)

would identify with the most—for one of the following characters: Walter, Beneatha, or Ruth. Each group should prepare for the debate by discussing among themselves what their character wants done with the money and why. The group members should also come up with some arguments in favor of their own plans for the money so that they can support their assertions. They also may want to try to anticipate how other teams will argue against them and how they might argue against the other teams' claims on the money.

After the groups have had time to meet, act as a moderator (you can pretend you are Mrs. Lena Younger, if you want; you can also have one student be a moderator rather than a group member, but the debate may be more effective with the teacher in charge) and get the debate going. Give each group a chance to speak, and then call on different groups to counter other groups' arguments. You may have to bring up particular issues or concerns to focus the debate. Try to encourage different group members to speak so that one person alone is not speaking for a given group all the time. (Practical/ Analytical)

- Instead of an oral debate, you can conduct a small-group persuasive writing exercise in which each group writes a separate persuasive letter to Lena Younger on behalf of their character. These letters can then be read aloud and discussed. (Practical/Analytical)
- Individually or in groups, the students can, acting as one of the characters in the play, write a letter to the editor of the local paper about an issue of concern to them. For example, the student(s) can be Walter writing about the difficulty of getting money to start a business as an African American man, or Lena describing the difficulty city residents face buying decent fruits and vegetables in their own neighborhoods, or Beneatha criticizing class snobbery within the African American community. (Practical/Analytical)
- As a class or in groups, the students can construct a business plan for a bookstore or toy store. You can provide them with some general categories of things to think about: store needs, monthly expenses, potential investors, ideal store location, layout of the store (perhaps one group of students can draw a floor plan after the store's needs have been considered), name of the store, what items the store will sell, employee training (what the employees will need to know/learn about the products), advertising (perhaps one group of students can design an ad for the store), and so on. Students can even come up with plans for a surrounding city block that will serve the needs of the community. (Practical/Creative)

UNIT LESSON 4: CREATIVE

Creative lessons are usually the most fun. They are fun to design and fun to observe. But these fun activities have serious objectives. The objectives of this lesson are to (a) build vocabulary, (b) enhance comprehension of the material, and (c) elicit the development of creative skills (suppose, pretend, think of). Following are various activities suggested for creative lessons.

Creating Environments

- Refocus the scene in which the Youngers' cramped quarters and cranky humor are in full display. Ask students to describe the Youngers' apartment and moods in the opening scene. Get them to understand the connection between the two. Try to get the students to connect this dynamic with their own personal experiences. Have they ever lived in a place with family that was just too small? Too old? Too loud? How does their home or school make them feel? Ask students to describe these places and the ways they felt there. (Creative/Analytical)
- Show students pictures of different environments. Use houses or buildings, interiors or exteriors of different sorts, parks, cities, farms, suburbs. Ask them to describe the mood, or the way they would feel there. (Creative/Analytical)
- Tell students that they're going to do an exercise in which they get to create an environment that has a particular effect. (This can be either an individual or a small-group exercise.) Use this as a writing or a drawing exercise (or both). The general idea is to assign, or let the students choose, a particular emotional state (excitement, boredom, comfort, depression, fear, tranquility, anger, or another) and then ask them to describe (in words or pictures, or both) either a place that makes them feel that way or an entirely imaginary place that, in their opinion, would produce that effect on the people who inhabited the space. Again, give the students time to work individually or in groups, and then regroup the class as a whole and ask students to share and talk about what they have written or drawn. (Creative/Analytical)

Other Possible Creative Activities

- Have the students create (on their own or in groups) imaginary character monologues. For example: If the ghost of Big Walter (Walter Sr.) came back to offer advice to his son Walter Lee, or to

(Continued)

(Continued)

> his wife Lena, what might he say? If Walter Lee could speak frankly to his employer, what might he tell him? If Beneatha were writing a personal essay for admission to medical school, what would she write? (Creative/Analytical)
>
> - You could set up a few scenes that do not happen in the play and then ask the students, either individually or in small groups, to write the scene (including dialogue between the characters). Some suggestions:
>
>   1. Lena Younger runs into Walter's boss, and the boss is rude to her.
>   2. Walter Lee gets a good job offer, but it's in a different state; he and Ruth debate what he should do.
>   3. Asagai asks Beneatha to forget about medical school, marry him, and become a revolutionary in Africa.
>
> - You could also ask the students to think of the setup for the scene themselves; they may very well come up with better ones than these. (Creative/Analytical)

UNIT HOMEWORK

If the length of your unit permits, it's a good idea to assign homework. Homework assignments are strongly recommended, and teachers are encouraged to use them as much as possible. In addition to being a great exercise tool, homework assignments put students in a situation of choice—they can decide for themselves whether they want to proceed with primarily analytical, creative, or practical assignments. The examples in this lesson are all home-based freewriting exercises. In addition, the following list (adapted from D. Lev, personal communication, 1998) shows how the writing process can be organized.

Writing Process

1. Interpret prompt (this process should take ten minutes for a short piece) (Analytical/Creative)

    Identify . . . (Analytical)

    Topic

    Purpose

    Audience

Brainstorm ideas in the form of a spider, cluster, or web (Creative)

Elaborate ideas by expanding a thought (Analytical/Creative)

Organize ideas; for example, number your ideas first, second, and so on (Practical)

2. Rough draft (this process should take twenty to thirty minutes for a short piece)

First, think . . .

Topic (Have you clearly stated your thoughts?)

Audience (To whom are you writing?)

Form (Is this a letter, speech, essay, argument, or poem?)

Now write ideas in some form

3. Revising ideas (Analytical/Practical)

Adding ideas

Deleting ideas

Expanding ideas or moving them around

4. Editing (Analytical)

Spelling

Punctuation

Grammar

Capitalization

5. Publishing (Practical)

Teachers can also give the following assignment to students.

Write (on a separate sheet of paper) your response to *one* of the following. (In other words, do A, B, *or* C.)

A. Lena Younger has asked you to advise her on how she should spend her $10,000. What would you suggest and why? (Practical)

B. Compare and contrast Lena's personality and character traits to those of her children, Walter Lee and Beneatha. In what ways are they similar and in what ways are they different? (Analytical)

(Continued)

(Continued)

> C. At one point in the screenplay, Beneatha tells Lena and Ruth, "People have to express themselves in one way or another." Pretend that you are one of the main characters in the screenplay. You are Walter, Ruth, Lena, or Beneatha, and you are going to write a letter sharing your thoughts, feelings, concerns, or dreams with another character in the play. Who would you like to be? Who would you write to? Write the letter. (Creative)

UNIT ASSESSMENT

Last but not least is assessment. Teachers are encouraged to assess their students on a regular basis. Note that assessment items match both the abilities that have been targeted by instructional materials and the format used in classroom activities. The first two items target practical ability, the second two target analytical ability, and the final two target creative ability.

> ### Comprehension Assessment
>
> For each question, circle the best answer or, if lines are provided, fill in your answer.
>
> 1. Which of the following actions would be the MOST likely to help Walter convince his mother, Lena Younger, to invest some of her money in his business ventures?
>   a. Walter could come up with a business idea that does not involve liquor.
>   b. Walter could ask Herman, the owner of the liquor store nearby, to talk to Lena.
>   c. Walter could lose his job on purpose; then Lena would have to give him the money.
>   d. Walter could demand that Beneatha marry George Murchison.
>
> 2. Walter and Beneatha argue a lot with one another. If the two of them asked your advice about how to get along better, what would you tell them?
>
> 3. Which of the following accurately describes a problem that Beneatha faces?
>   a. Her grandmother does not look kindly on her desire to attend medical school.

b. She is not smart enough to become a doctor.

c. Men sometimes discourage her dreams or laugh at her ideas because she is a woman.

d. She depends on God too much instead of doing things for herself.

4. Explain why the little plant is included in the story from time to time. In other words, what would you say the plant symbolizes or represents?

5. In one scene, Walter Younger, in his chauffeur uniform, stares intently at himself in the mirror as a bell tinkles in the background to summon him. What do you suppose Walter is thinking at that moment?

6. Pretend that you are designing a new (but not extravagant or grand) house for the Youngers. Taking into account what you know about the different family members (their needs and interests), what features would the house have?

CONCLUSION

This is an example of how others have conducted TIA. Now you're ready to try it. We're confident that it will work in your classroom, just as it has worked for so many other teachers.

RESOURCES

Grade Level Activities

Grade Level	Language Arts	Mathematics	Science	Social Studies	Foreign Language	Art	Music	Physical Education
Primary Grades K–4	Lesson 5	Lesson 1	Lesson 4	Lesson 8	Lesson 6	Lesson 1	Lesson 1	Lesson 3
	Lesson 6	Lesson 6	Lesson 6	Lesson 9	Lesson 11	Lesson 2	Lesson 2	Lesson 4
	Lesson 10	Lesson 8	Lesson 9	Lesson 14	Lesson 16	Lesson 3	Lesson 4	Lesson 5
	Lesson 11	Lesson 10	Lesson 11	Lesson 17	Lesson 38	Lesson 4	Lesson 6	Lesson 8
	Lesson 14	Lesson 11	Lesson 13	Lesson 24		Lesson 5	Lesson 8	Lesson 9
	Lesson 17	Lesson 12	Lesson 15	Lesson 25		Lesson 8	Lesson 9	Lesson 10
	Lesson 21	Lesson 15	Lesson 17	Lesson 32		Lesson 11	Lesson 11	Lesson 11
	Lesson 22	Lesson 21	Lesson 18	Lesson 34		Lesson 13	Lesson 13	Lesson 12
	Lesson 29	Lesson 22	Lesson 19	Lesson 36		Lesson 14	Lesson 16	Lesson 13
	Lesson 31	Lesson 25	Lesson 21	Lesson 37		Lesson 15	Lesson 17	Lesson 14
	Lesson 32	Lesson 26	Lesson 28	Lesson 39		Lesson 18	Lesson 19	Lesson 15
	Lesson 34	Lesson 29	Lesson 30			Lesson 19	Lesson 21	Lesson 17
	Lesson 35	Lesson 34	Lesson 33			Lesson 22	Lesson 22	Lesson 18
	Lesson 37	Lesson 35	Lesson 35			Lesson 25	Lesson 24	Lesson 19
	Lesson 39	Lesson 37				Lesson 26	Lesson 27	Lesson 21
		Lesson 39				Lesson 27	Lesson 30	Lesson 22
						Lesson 28	Lesson 32	Lesson 23
						Lesson 29	Lesson 35	Lesson 24
						Lesson 31	Lesson 37	Lesson 27
						Lesson 35	Lesson 39	Lesson 32
						Lesson 38		Lesson 33
								Lesson 34
								Lesson 35
								Lesson 36
								Lesson 38
								Lesson 39

Grade Level	Language Arts	Mathematics	Science	Social Studies	Foreign Language	Art	Music	Physical Education
Intermediate Grades 5–8	Lesson 1 Lesson 3 Lesson 5 Lesson 6 Lesson 8 Lesson 9 Lesson 10 Lesson 11 Lesson 13 Lesson 14 Lesson 15 Lesson 16 Lesson 17 Lesson 18 Lesson 19 Lesson 21 Lesson 22 Lesson 23 Lesson 24 Lesson 26 Lesson 27 Lesson 28 Lesson 29 Lesson 30 Lesson 31 Lesson 33 Lesson 34 Lesson 35 Lesson 37 Lesson 39	Lesson 1 Lesson 2 Lesson 4 Lesson 6 Lesson 8 Lesson 10 Lesson 11 Lesson 12 Lesson 13 Lesson 15 Lesson 17 Lesson 21 Lesson 22 Lesson 25 Lesson 26 Lesson 29 Lesson 30 Lesson 31 Lesson 32 Lesson 33 Lesson 34 Lesson 35 Lesson 36 Lesson 37 Lesson 39	Lesson 1 Lesson 2 Lesson 4 Lesson 6 Lesson 9 Lesson 10 Lesson 11 Lesson 13 Lesson 17 Lesson 18 Lesson 19 Lesson 21 Lesson 23 Lesson 27 Lesson 29 Lesson 30 Lesson 31 Lesson 33 Lesson 34 Lesson 35 Lesson 38	Lesson 1 Lesson 4 Lesson 5 Lesson 8 Lesson 9 Lesson 10 Lesson 11 Lesson 13 Lesson 14 Lesson 19 Lesson 22 Lesson 23 Lesson 24 Lesson 25 Lesson 28 Lesson 29 Lesson 31 Lesson 32 Lesson 34 Lesson 36 Lesson 37 Lesson 38 Lesson 39	Lesson 2 Lesson 3 Lesson 4 Lesson 5 Lesson 6 Lesson 9 Lesson 11 Lesson 13 Lesson 15 Lesson 16 Lesson 17 Lesson 18 Lesson 19 Lesson 22 Lesson 23 Lesson 24 Lesson 25 Lesson 26 Lesson 27 Lesson 28 Lesson 30 Lesson 31 Lesson 33 Lesson 34 Lesson 35 Lesson 37 Lesson 38 Lesson 39	Lesson 1 Lesson 2 Lesson 3 Lesson 4 Lesson 5 Lesson 6 Lesson 8 Lesson 10 Lesson 11 Lesson 12 Lesson 14 Lesson 15 Lesson 16 Lesson 17 Lesson 18 Lesson 21 Lesson 22 Lesson 23 Lesson 29 Lesson 31 Lesson 32 Lesson 34 Lesson 35 Lesson 37 Lesson 38 Lesson 39	Lesson 2 Lesson 3 Lesson 4 Lesson 6 Lesson 8 Lesson 9 Lesson 11 Lesson 13 Lesson 14 Lesson 15 Lesson 16 Lesson 17 Lesson 18 Lesson 19 Lesson 21 Lesson 22 Lesson 23 Lesson 24 Lesson 25 Lesson 26 Lesson 27 Lesson 28 Lesson 29 Lesson 31 Lesson 32 Lesson 33 Lesson 34 Lesson 35 Lesson 36 Lesson 37 Lesson 38 Lesson 39	Lesson 1 Lesson 2 Lesson 3 Lesson 4 Lesson 5 Lesson 8 Lesson 9 Lesson 10 Lesson 11 Lesson 12 Lesson 13 Lesson 14 Lesson 15 Lesson 18 Lesson 19 Lesson 21 Lesson 22 Lesson 23 Lesson 24 Lesson 26 Lesson 27 Lesson 29 Lesson 30 Lesson 32 Lesson 33 Lesson 34 Lesson 35 Lesson 36 Lesson 37 Lesson 38 Lesson 39

Grade Level	Language Arts	Mathematics	Science	Social Studies	Foreign Language	Art	Music	Physical Education
High School Grades 9–12	Lesson 2	Lesson 1	Lesson 1	Lesson 1	Lesson 1	Lesson 2	Lesson 3	Lesson 1
	Lesson 3	Lesson 2	Lesson 2	Lesson 2	Lesson 2	Lesson 3	Lesson 4	Lesson 2
	Lesson 4	Lesson 3	Lesson 3	Lesson 4	Lesson 3	Lesson 8	Lesson 5	Lesson 4
	Lesson 5	Lesson 4	Lesson 4	Lesson 5	Lesson 4	Lesson 9	Lesson 6	Lesson 5
	Lesson 6	Lesson 5	Lesson 5	Lesson 6	Lesson 5	Lesson 10	Lesson 9	Lesson 6
	Lesson 8	Lesson 6	Lesson 6	Lesson 8	Lesson 6	Lesson 11	Lesson 10	Lesson 8
	Lesson 9	Lesson 8	Lesson 10	Lesson 9	Lesson 8	Lesson 12	Lesson 12	Lesson 9
	Lesson 11	Lesson 9	Lesson 11	Lesson 10	Lesson 9	Lesson 14	Lesson 14	Lesson 12
	Lesson 12	Lesson 10	Lesson 12	Lesson 12	Lesson 10	Lesson 16	Lesson 15	Lesson 13
	Lesson 13	Lesson 11	Lesson 13	Lesson 13	Lesson 12	Lesson 21	Lesson 16	Lesson 14
	Lesson 15	Lesson 12	Lesson 14	Lesson 14	Lesson 13	Lesson 23	Lesson 17	Lesson 16
	Lesson 16	Lesson 14	Lesson 16	Lesson 15	Lesson 14	Lesson 24	Lesson 18	Lesson 18
	Lesson 18	Lesson 15	Lesson 17	Lesson 16	Lesson 15	Lesson 29	Lesson 21	Lesson 21
	Lesson 19	Lesson 16	Lesson 21	Lesson 18	Lesson 16	Lesson 30	Lesson 22	Lesson 22
	Lesson 22	Lesson 17	Lesson 23	Lesson 19	Lesson 17	Lesson 31	Lesson 23	Lesson 23
	Lesson 23	Lesson 18	Lesson 25	Lesson 21	Lesson 18	Lesson 32	Lesson 25	Lesson 24
	Lesson 24	Lesson 19	Lesson 26	Lesson 22	Lesson 19	Lesson 33	Lesson 26	Lesson 25
	Lesson 25	Lesson 21	Lesson 27	Lesson 23	Lesson 21	Lesson 34	Lesson 27	Lesson 26
	Lesson 26	Lesson 22	Lesson 29	Lesson 24	Lesson 22	Lesson 36	Lesson 28	Lesson 27
	Lesson 27	Lesson 23	Lesson 30	Lesson 25	Lesson 23	Lesson 37	Lesson 31	Lesson 28
	Lesson 28	Lesson 24	Lesson 31	Lesson 26	Lesson 24	Lesson 38	Lesson 32	Lesson 29
	Lesson 29	Lesson 25	Lesson 32	Lesson 27	Lesson 25	Lesson 39	Lesson 33	Lesson 30
	Lesson 33	Lesson 26	Lesson 34	Lesson 28	Lesson 26		Lesson 34	Lesson 31
	Lesson 34	Lesson 27	Lesson 35	Lesson 29	Lesson 27		Lesson 35	Lesson 32
	Lesson 35	Lesson 28	Lesson 37	Lesson 30	Lesson 28		Lesson 36	Lesson 34
	Lesson 36	Lesson 29	Lesson 38	Lesson 31	Lesson 29		Lesson 37	Lesson 35
	Lesson 37	Lesson 30	Lesson 39	Lesson 32	Lesson 30		Lesson 38	Lesson 36
	Lesson 38	Lesson 31		Lesson 33	Lesson 31		Lesson 39	Lesson 37
	Lesson 39	Lesson 32		Lesson 34	Lesson 32			Lesson 38
		Lesson 33		Lesson 35	Lesson 33			Lesson 39
		Lesson 34		Lesson 36	Lesson 34			
		Lesson 35		Lesson 37	Lesson 35			
		Lesson 36		Lesson 38	Lesson 36			
		Lesson 37		Lesson 39	Lesson 37			
		Lesson 38			Lesson 38			
		Lesson 39			Lesson 39			

Grade Level	Language Arts	Mathematics	Science	Social Studies	Foreign Language	Art	Music	Physical Education
College	Lesson 2	Lesson 1	Lesson 1	Lesson 1	Lesson 1	Lesson 2	Lesson 3	Lesson 1
	Lesson 3	Lesson 2	Lesson 2	Lesson 2	Lesson 2	Lesson 3	Lesson 4	Lesson 2
	Lesson 4	Lesson 3	Lesson 3	Lesson 4	Lesson 3	Lesson 8	Lesson 5	Lesson 4
	Lesson 5	Lesson 4	Lesson 4	Lesson 5	Lesson 5	Lesson 10	Lesson 6	Lesson 5
	Lesson 6	Lesson 5	Lesson 5	Lesson 6	Lesson 6	Lesson 11	Lesson 9	Lesson 6
	Lesson 8	Lesson 6	Lesson 6	Lesson 8	Lesson 8	Lesson 12	Lesson 10	Lesson 8
	Lesson 9	Lesson 8	Lesson 10	Lesson 9	Lesson 9	Lesson 14	Lesson 12	Lesson 9
	Lesson 11	Lesson 9	Lesson 11	Lesson 10	Lesson 10	Lesson 16	Lesson 14	Lesson 12
	Lesson 12	Lesson 10	Lesson 12	Lesson 12	Lesson 12	Lesson 21	Lesson 15	Lesson 13
	Lesson 13	Lesson 11	Lesson 13	Lesson 13	Lesson 13	Lesson 23	Lesson 16	Lesson 14
	Lesson 15	Lesson 12	Lesson 14	Lesson 14	Lesson 14	Lesson 24	Lesson 17	Lesson 16
	Lesson 16	Lesson 14	Lesson 16	Lesson 15	Lesson 15	Lesson 29	Lesson 18	Lesson 18
	Lesson 18	Lesson 15	Lesson 17	Lesson 16	Lesson 16	Lesson 30	Lesson 21	Lesson 21
	Lesson 19	Lesson 16	Lesson 21	Lesson 18	Lesson 17	Lesson 31	Lesson 22	Lesson 22
	Lesson 22	Lesson 17	Lesson 23	Lesson 19	Lesson 18	Lesson 32	Lesson 23	Lesson 23
	Lesson 23	Lesson 18	Lesson 25	Lesson 21	Lesson 19	Lesson 33	Lesson 25	Lesson 24
	Lesson 24	Lesson 19	Lesson 26	Lesson 22	Lesson 21	Lesson 34	Lesson 26	Lesson 25
	Lesson 25	Lesson 21	Lesson 27	Lesson 23	Lesson 22	Lesson 35	Lesson 27	Lesson 26
	Lesson 26	Lesson 22	Lesson 29	Lesson 24	Lesson 23	Lesson 36	Lesson 28	Lesson 27
	Lesson 27	Lesson 23	Lesson 30	Lesson 25	Lesson 25	Lesson 37	Lesson 31	Lesson 28
	Lesson 28	Lesson 24	Lesson 31	Lesson 26	Lesson 26	Lesson 38	Lesson 32	Lesson 29
	Lesson 29	Lesson 25	Lesson 32	Lesson 27	Lesson 27	Lesson 39	Lesson 33	Lesson 30
	Lesson 33	Lesson 26	Lesson 34	Lesson 28	Lesson 28		Lesson 34	Lesson 31
	Lesson 34	Lesson 27	Lesson 35	Lesson 29	Lesson 29		Lesson 35	Lesson 32
	Lesson 35	Lesson 28	Lesson 37	Lesson 30	Lesson 30		Lesson 36	Lesson 34
	Lesson 36	Lesson 29	Lesson 38	Lesson 31	Lesson 31		Lesson 37	Lesson 35
	Lesson 37	Lesson 30	Lesson 39	Lesson 32	Lesson 32		Lesson 38	Lesson 36
	Lesson 38	Lesson 31		Lesson 33	Lesson 33		Lesson 39	Lesson 37
	Lesson 39	Lesson 32		Lesson 34	Lesson 34			Lesson 38
		Lesson 33		Lesson 35	Lesson 35			Lesson 39
		Lesson 34		Lesson 36	Lesson 36			
		Lesson 35		Lesson 37	Lesson 37			
		Lesson 36		Lesson 38	Lesson 38			
		Lesson 37		Lesson 39	Lesson 39			
		Lesson 38						
		Lesson 39						

Note: See also Lessons 7 (p. 53), 20 (p. 87), and 40 (p. 131) for additional activities in each content area.

References

Introduction

Grigorenko, E. L., Jarvin, L., & Sternberg, R. J. (2002). School-based tests of the triarchic theory of intelligence: Three settings, three samples, three syllabi. *Contemporary Educational Psychology, 27,* 167–208.

Sternberg, R. J. (1997). *Successful intelligence.* New York: Plume.

Sternberg, R. J. (1999). The theory of successful intelligence. *Review of General Psychology, 3,* 292–316.

Sternberg, R. J. (2002). Raising the achievement of all students: Teaching for successful intelligence. *Educational Psychology Review, 14,* 383–393.

Sternberg, R. J., Grigorenko, E. L., Ferrari, M., & Clinkenbeard, P. (1999). A triarchic analysis of an aptitude-treatment interaction. *European Journal of Psychological Assessment, 15*(1), 1–11.

Sternberg, R. J., Grigorenko, E. L., & Jarvin, L. (2001). Improving reading instruction: The triarchic model. *Educational Leadership, 58*(6), 48–52.

Sternberg, R. J., Torff, B., & Grigorenko, E. L. (1998a). Teaching for successful intelligence raises school achievement. *Phi Delta Kappan, 79*(9), 667–669.

Sternberg, R. J., Torff, B., & Grigorenko, E. L. (1998b). Teaching triarchically improves school achievement. *Journal of Educational Psychology, 90*(3), 1–11.

Chapter 1: What Is Successful Intelligence?

Adams, M. J. (1990). *Beginning to read: Thinking and learning about print.* Cambridge: MIT Press.

Binet, A., & Simon, T. (1916). The development of intelligence in children. Baltimore: Williams & Wilkins.

Stanovich, K. E. (1999). Romance and reality. In Consortium on Reading Excellence (Ed.), *Reading research anthology: The why? of reading instruction* (pp. 24–25). Novato, CA: Arena Press.

Sternberg, R. J., & Grigorenko, E. L. (1999). Myths in psychology and education regarding the gene-environment debate. *Teachers College Record, 100,* 536–553.

Sternberg, R. J., & Spear-Swerling, L. (1996). *Teaching for thinking.* Washington, DC: American Psychological Association.

Wechsler, D. (1939). *The measure of adult intelligence.* Baltimore: Williams & Wilkins.

Chapter 2: Examining the Theory of Successful Intelligence

Binet, A., & Simon, T. (1916). *The development of intelligence in children*. Baltimore: Williams & Wilkins.

Fraser, S. (Ed.). (1995). *The bell curve wars: Race, intelligence and the future of America*. New York: Basic Books.

Hernnstein, R. J., & Murray, C. (1994). *The bell curve*. New York: Free Press.

Jacoby, R., & Glauberman, N. (Eds.). (1995). *The bell curve debate*. New York: Time Books.

Stephenson, L. S. (2001). Optimizing the benefits of anthelmintic treatment in children. *Paediatric Drugs, 3*, 495–508.

Sternberg, R. J. (1995). *In search of the human mind*. Orlando, FL: Harcourt Brace College.

Sternberg, R. J. (1998). *Love is a story*. New York: Oxford University Press.

Sternberg, R. J., Ferrari, M., Clinkenbeard, P. R., & Grigorenko, E. L. (1996). Identification, instruction, and assessment of gifted children: A construct validation of a triarchic model. *Gifted Child Quarterly, 40*, 129–137.

Sternberg, R. J., Grigorenko, E. L., Ferrari, M., & Clinkenbeard, P. (1999). A triarchic analysis of an aptitude-treatment interaction. *European Journal of Psychological Assessment, 15*, 1–11.

Sternberg, R. J., Powell, C., McGrane, P. A., & Grantham-McGregor, S. (1997). Effects of a parasitic infection on cognitive functioning. *Journal of Experimental Psychology: Applied, 3*, 67–76.

Sternberg, R. J., Torff, B., & Grigorenko, E. L. (1998a). Teaching for successful intelligence raises school achievement. *Phi Delta Kappan, 79*(9), 667–669.

Sternberg, R. J., Torff, B., & Grigorenko, E. L. (1998b). Teaching triarchically improves school achievement. *Journal of Educational Psychology, 90*(3), 1–11.

Chapter 3: Successful Intelligence in Life and in School

Carraher, T. N., Carraher, D., & Schliemann, A. D. (1985). Mathematics in the streets and in schools. *British Journal of Developmental Psychology, 3*, 21–29.

Ceci, S. J., & Roazzi, A. (1994). The effects of context on cognition: Postcards from Brazil. In R. J. Sternberg & R. K. Wagner (Eds.), *Mind in context: Interactionist perspectives on human intelligence* (pp. 74–101). New York: Cambridge University Press.

Cole, M., Gay, J., Glick, J., & Sharp, D. W. (1971). *The cultural context of learning and thinking*. New York: Basic Books.

Lave, J. (1988). *Cognition in practice*. New York: Cambridge University Press.

Nuñes, T. (1994). Street intelligence. In R. J. Sternberg (Ed.), *Encyclopedia of human intelligence* (Vol. 2, pp. 1045–1049). New York: Macmillan.

Okagaki, L., & Sternberg, R. J. (1993). Parental beliefs and children's school performance. *Child Development, 64*(1), 36–56.

Rogoff, B. (1990). *Apprenticeship in thinking: Cognitive development in social context*. New York: Oxford University Press.

Sennet, R. (1998). *The corrosion of character*. New York: Norton.

Steele, C. M., & Aronson, J. (1995). Stereotype threats and the intellectual test performance of African Americans. *Journal of Personality and Social Psychology, 69*, 797–811.

Sternberg, R. J. (2004). Culture and intelligence. *American Psychologist, 59*(5), 325–338.

Sternberg, R. J., Forsythe, G. B., Hedlund, J., Horvath, J., Snook, S., Williams, W. M., et al. (2000). *Practical intelligence in everyday life*. New York: Cambridge University Press.

Sternberg, R. J., & Grigorenko, E. L. (1997). The cognitive costs of physical and mental ill health: Applying the psychology of the developed world to the problems of the developing world. *Eye on Psi Chi, 2*(1), 20–27.

Sternberg, R. J., Nokes, K., Geissler, P. W., Prince, R., Okatcha, F., Bundy, D. A., et al. (2001). The relationship between academic and practical intelligence: A case study in Kenya. *Intelligence, 29*, 401–418.

Chapter 4: Teaching for Analytical Thinking

Associated Press. (2007, February 23). *Pakistan successfully tests long-range nuclear-capable missile*. Retrieved February 26, 2007, from http://www.fox news.com/story/0,2933,253918,00.html

Sacks, O. (1985). *The man who mistook his wife for a hat and other clinical tales*. New York: Touchstone.

Sternberg, R. J. (1977). *Intelligence, information processing, and analogical reasoning: The componential analysis of human abilities*. Hillsdale, NJ: Lawrence Erlbaum.

Sternberg, R. J. (1979). The nature of mental abilities. *American Psychologist, 34*, 214–230.

Sternberg, R. J. (1980a). The development of linear syllogistic reasoning. *Journal of Experimental Child Psychology, 29*, 340–356.

Sternberg, R. J. (1980b). Representation and process in linear syllogistic reasoning. *Journal of Experimental Psychology: General, 109*, 119–159.

Sternberg, R. J. (1981a). Intelligence and nonentrenchment. *Journal of Educational Psychology, 73*, 1–16.

Sternberg, R. J. (1981b). Intelligence as thinking and learning skills. *Educational Leadership, 39*(1), 18–20.

Sternberg, R. J. (1985). *Beyond IQ: A triarchic theory of human intelligence*. New York: Cambridge University Press.

Sternberg, R. J. (1998). *Love is a story*. New York: Oxford University Press.

Sternberg, R. J. (2006). *Cognitive psychology* (4th ed.). Forth Worth, TX: Harcourt Brace College.

Sternberg, R. J., & Bhana, K. (1986). Synthesis of research on the effectiveness of intellectual skills programs: Snake-oil remedies or miracle cures? *Educational Leadership, 44*(2), 60–67.

Wagner, R. K., & Sternberg, R. J. (1987). Executive control in reading comprehension. In B. K. Britton & S. M. Glynn (Eds.), *Executive control processes in reading* (pp. 1–21). Hillsdale, NJ: Lawrence Erlbaum.

Chapter 5: Teaching for Creative Thinking

Amabile, T. M. (1996). *Creativity in context*. Boulder, CO: Westview.

Dewey, J. (1933). *How we think*. Boston: Heath.

Frensch, P. A., & Sternberg, R. J. (1989). Expertise and intelligent thinking: When is it worse to know better? In R. J. Sternberg (Ed.), *Advances in the psychology of human intelligence* (Vol. 5, pp. 157–158). Hillsdale, NJ: Lawrence Erlbaum.

Garcia, J., & Koelling, R. A. (1966). The relation of cue to consequence in avoidance learning. *Psychonomic Science, 4*, 123–124.

Gruber, H. E., & Davis, S. N. (1988). Inching our way up Mount Olympus: The evolving-systems approach to creative thinking. In R. J. Sternberg (Ed.), *The nature of creativity* (pp. 243–270). New York: Cambridge University Press.

Lucas, V. [S. Plath]. (1963). *The bell jar*. London: Heinemann.

Morrison, T. (1982). *Tar baby*. New York: Vintage Books.

Schank, R. C. (1988). *The creative attitude*. New York: Macmillan.

Sternberg, R. J. (1985). *Beyond IQ: A triarchic theory of human intelligence*. New York: Cambridge University Press.

Sternberg, R. J. (1986). *Intelligence applied. Understanding and increasing your intellectual skills*. San Diego, CA: Harcourt Brace Jovanovich.

Sternberg, R. J. (1997a). *Successful intelligence*. New York: Plume.

Sternberg, R. J. (1997b). *Thinking styles*. New York: Cambridge University Press.

Sternberg, R. J., Kaufman, J. A., & Grigorenko, E. L. (2007). *Intelligence applied* (2nd ed.). New York: Cambridge University Press.

Sternberg, R. J., & Lubart, T. I. (1995a). *Defying the crowd: Cultivating creativity in a culture of conformity*. New York: Free Press.

Sternberg, R. J., & Lubart, T. I. (1995b). Ten tips toward creativity in the workplace. In C. M. Ford & D. A. Gioia (Eds.), *Creative action in organizations: Ivory tower visions and real world voices* (pp. 173–180). Newbury Park, CA: Sage.

Sternberg, R. J., & O'Hara, L. (1999). Creativity and intelligence. In R. J. Sternberg (Ed.), *Handbook of creativity* (pp. 251–272). New York: Cambridge University Press.

Sternberg, R. J., & Williams, W. M. (1996). *How to develop student creativity*. Alexandria, VA: Association for Supervision and Curriculum Development.

Chapter 6: Teaching for Practical Thinking

Amabile, T. M. (1996). *Creativity in context*. Boulder, CO: Westview.

Csikszentmihalyi, M. (1988). Society, culture, and person: A systems view of creativity. In R. J. Sternberg (Ed.), *Nature of creativity* (pp. 325–339). New York: Cambridge University Press.

Gardner, H. (1993). *Creating minds*. New York: Basic Books.

Stenhouse, D. (1973). *The evolution of intelligence: A general theory and some of its implications*. New York: Harper & Row.

Steptoe, A. (Ed.). (1998). *Genius and the mind*. New York: Oxford University Press.

Sternberg, R. J. (1986). *Intelligence applied: Understanding and increasing your intellectual skills*. San Diego, CA: Harcourt Brace Jovanovich.

Sternberg, R. J. (1999). The theory of successful intelligence. *Review of General Psychology, 3*, 292–316.

Sternberg, R. J., & Lubart, T. I. (1995). *Defying the crowd: Cultivating creativity in a culture of conformity.* New York: Free Press.

Sternberg, R. J., & Spear-Swerling, L. (1996). *Teaching for thinking.* Washington, DC: American Psychological Association.

Stevenson, H., & Stigler, J. (1994). *The learning gap.* New York: Simon & Schuster.

Thurstone, L. L. (1924). *The nature of intelligence.* New York: Harcourt Brace.

Winner, E. (1998). *Gifted children.* New York: Basic Books.

Chapter 7: Framing Triarchic Instruction and Assessment Units

Farr, R. C., & Strickland, D. S. (1993). *Light up the sky.* Orlando, FL: Harcourt Brace Jovanovich.

Grigorenko, E. L., Jarvin, L., & Sternberg, R. J. (2002). School-based tests of the triarchic theory of intelligence: Three settings, three samples, three syllabi. *Contemporary Educational Psychology, 27,* 167–208.

Hunt, I. (1992). *The lottery rose.* Madison, WI: Turtleback.

O'Hara, L. A., & Sternberg, R. J. (2000–2001). It doesn't hurt to ask: Effects of instructions to be creative, practical, or analytical on essay-writing performance and their interaction with students' thinking styles. *Creativity Research Journal, 13*(2), 197–210.

Stemler, S. E., Elliott, J. G., Grigorenko, E. L., & Sternberg, R. J. (2006). There's more to teaching than instruction: Seven strategies for dealing with the practical side of teaching. *Educational Studies, 32*(1), 101–118.

Sternberg, R. J. (2002). Raising the achievement of all students: Teaching for successful intelligence. *Educational Psychology Review, 14,* 383–393.

Sternberg, R. J. (2003). Teaching for successful intelligence: Principles, practices, and outcomes. *Educational and Child Psychology, 20*(2), 6–18.

Sternberg, R. J. (2006). Successful intelligence: Toward a broader model for teaching and accountability. *Edge, 1*(5), 2–18.

Sternberg, R. J., & Grigorenko, E. L. (2002). The theory of successful intelligence as a basis for instruction and assessment in higher education. In D. Halpern & M. Hakel (Eds.), *Applying the science of learning to university teaching and beyond: New directions for teaching and learning, No. 89.* San Francisco: Jossey-Bass.

Sternberg, R. J., & Williams, W. M. (2001). Teaching for creativity: Two dozen tips. In R. D. Small & A. P Thomas (Eds.), *Plain talk about education* (pp. 153–165). Covington, LA: Center for Development and Learning.

Chapter 8: Putting It All together: A Comprehensive Illustration of Lessons for Teaching for Successful Intelligence

Hansberry, L. (1994). *A raisin in the sun.* New York: Penguin.

Index